MW00461223

BEHIND THE SCENES

Improvising Long Form

MICK NAPIER

MERIWETHER PUBLISHING
A division of Pioneer Drama Service, Inc.
Denver, Colorado

Meriwether Publishing
A division of Pioneer Drama Service, Inc.
PO Box 4267
Englewood, CO 80155

www.pioneerdrama.com

Editor: Rebecca Johnson
Cover design: Devin Watson
Interior design: Damonza
Project manager: Karen Bullock

Printed in the United States of America
First Edition

ISBN: 978-1-56608-199-3

Library of Congress Cataloging-in-Publication Data

Names: Napier, Mick.
Title: Behind the scenes : improvising long form / Mick Napier ; with a foreword by Bob Odenkirk.
Description: Englewood, CO : Meriwether Publishing, [2015]
Identifiers: LCCN 2015040361 | ISBN 9781566081993 (pbk. : alk. paper)
Subjects: LCSH: Improvisation (Acting)
Classification: LCC PN2071.I5 N349 2015 | DDC 792.02/8—dc23
LC record available at http://lccn.loc.gov/2015040361

1 2 3   15 16 17

To Jennifer Estlin, who is everything to me.

For my mother, Pat Napier, whom I love dearly.

CONTENTS

FOREWORD BY BOB ODENKIRK

"Napier the Great and Powerful"
A legend in Chicago improv and theatre…
A mysterious figure spoken of in whispers and lies…
Mick has been the catalyst for the most messed-up, funny, smart, low-budget, loud, subversive, hilarious, mind-expanding improv (and scripted) shows of his time (that would be my time, too). Also, because he has directed for The Second City, he knows—and cares about—how to please an audience. He can do both: challenge and satisfy. He's like the roughest Swedish masseuse ever, but with a happy ending. That's called a "double-whammy" for the next time you're getting a massage.

This here book has got just what you want—a great teacher opening up his mind and letting us in on the knowledge of a lifetime of observing and pushing boundaries. The craziest thing about it all is how not-crazy it is: the lessons are straightforward and address the most down-to-earth aspects of taking a stage and making up a character and show. Where's the sorcery? I mean, if Mick wants to hang onto his dangerous, quasi-mystical reputation, shouldn't he be throwing a bunch of circumlocutory hogwash at us, daring the reader to try to make sense of it, and making us all feel small and stupid and a little scared? He should. Good thing he didn't consult with me before writing this tome.

Here's his problem: he's the real deal. He really loves improv, and he really wants you to get better at thinking about it. He has no need to obfuscate or put on a bullshit show. He's not afraid to speak plainly about the real challenges of improvising well and for its real purpose: entertainment. His observations here are simpler and more straightforward than you would have guessed, but still eminently hard to execute. Mick points to what really matters in approaching this kind of work—what to think about and how to understand what is being pursued—and he will make you laugh while doing it.

In this book, the Great and Powerful Napier shares it all about a life-long pursuit. He can be casual and even caustic with his opinion, almost disrespectful. But that's his prerogative because his love is so deep and unquestionable that he can afford to be brutally honest. Makes me want to break out in song: "Mick and Improv, sittin' in a tree…"

Save yourself a couple years of pain and struggle and read this book and take it seriously. It's the real deal, and so is Mick.

Bob Odenkirk is a goddamn busybody. An Emmy-winning Saturday Night Live *writer for eight seasons, he is best known for* Mr. Show with Bob and David, *along with his portrayal of Saul Goodman on AMC's Emmy-nominated* Breaking Bad. *The spinoff series,* Better Call Saul, *earned Odenkirk an Emmy nomination for best lead actor.*

ACKNOWLEDGMENTS

I would like to thank: Jennifer Estlin, who helps me edit and make sense of my words. She is the love of my life. My mother, Pat, who has been a constant support over these many years. My brother, Mark, the very best brother I could have and his wonderful wife, Lisa. My father, Fred, for his support and humor through the years. Jennifer's parents, Judy and Richard, for their love, as well as her brothers, Jonathan and David, and her sister, Rachel. A very special thanks to Uncle Jim Rosenblum, who has an unbelievable heart. My friend, my sister, Lyn Pusztai, for so many things... especially for making the theater beautiful.

Thank you to my Second City family for always supporting me—Andrew Alexander, Kelly Leonard, Beth Kligerman, Alison Riley, Robin Johnson, Monica Wilson, Jenna Deja, Craig Taylor, Jeremy Smith, Joyce and Cheryl Sloane, Sheldon Patinkin, and Martin deMaat.

Alan Myerson, who first created long form with The Committee. Charna Halpern and Del Close, who evolved The Harold and created iO. Matt Besser, Matt Walsh, Amy Poehler, and Ian Roberts, who masterfully grew long form and created UCB.

Stephen Colbert and Bob Odenkirk for their friendship and forewords. Adam Rubin, Mantas Dumcius, and Jeff Quintana, for reading first drafts and providing valuable feedback. Pioneer Drama and my editors, and especially Karen Bullock, who has been a pleasure to work with and who helped bring this book to life. Philip Markle for his feedback, and for helping to create The Annoyance in Brooklyn, NY.

To all of the creators of *Trigger Happy* for making this 20-year dream come true: Sarah Ashley, Ryan Asher, Alison Banowsky, Danny Catlow, Tyler Davis, Susan Glynn, Katie Kershaw, Eve Krueger, Tim Lamphier, Max Lipchitz, Molly Miller, Vernon Mina, Jillian Mueller, Greg Ott, Bruce Phillips, CJ Tuor, Griffin Wenzler, and Alex Young.

The wonderful staff of The Annoyance in Chicago: Chelsea Rendlen, Duke Harbison, Pete Pereira, Chris Kervick, Tom Troup, Evan Mills, Nick Bell, Elijah Barnes, and Smith Powell.

To my dear friends and Annoyance founders and veterans: Susan Messing, Mark Sutton, Ellen Stoneking, Lisa McQueen, Rich Sohn, and Rebecca Sohn.

To the caring and amazing teachers of The Annoyance: Derrick Aguis, Lilly Allison, Katie Caussin, Charley Carroll, Sean Cusick, Kyle Dolan, Wolfgang Stein, Irene Marquette, Jimmy Pennington, Jo Scott, Megan Johns, Tim McKendrick, and Michael McCarthy.

And lastly, thank you to all of the actors, directors, musicians, technicians, and improvisers in the history of The Annoyance.

1

WHAT IS LONG FORM IMPROVISATION?

Long form. Simple.

Take a suggestion.

Improvise with some people for a half hour to an hour based on that suggestion.

Simple.

Not so simple.

Although implied in its name, the length of a long form improvisation is not nearly as definitive to the genre as the actors' approach to the audience's contribution. The fact that the actors can improvise for such an extended period on a single proposition is what truly separates long form from other types of improvisation. Granted, in traditional improv games, the suggestion alone is what drives the improvisation. Half the fun for the audience is the ensemble's ability to navigate, accommodate, and create comedy from their input right on the spot. However, in long form, the actors use the suggestion garnered from the audience to explore both form and content throughout their improvisational journey. The suggestion is certainly attended to, but it primarily provides an overriding theme or inspiration for a more freely improvised piece that has the ability to play for a more extended period of time.

As in short form improvisation (formerly known as improv games), which usually lasts anywhere from four to ten minutes, long form comes in many different incarnations or, well, forms. There are Harolds, montages, deconstructions, La Rondes, Living Rooms, Triggers, improvised movies, and improvised one-acts. Even a single improvised scene between two people could be classified as long form if it adheres to a single suggestion and lasts more than ten minutes or so. It is the unique combination of the length of time and the use of a single suggestion that is the essence of long form. All improv is, of course, is making up things on the spot, but improv becomes long form when these two criteria are in play.

Long form ensembles around the world are usually comprised of six to ten people, although it can be more or less depending on the type of long form employed. Ensemble members often enjoy long form improvisation more than traditional improv because of the freedom it provides. Inspired but not restricted by the single suggestion, improvisers feel more free to explore, play, and create an entire piece with only themselves and their fellow ensemble members. They are unrestrained by the need to closely attend to the audience's suggestion, which is required in short form.

Similarly, an audience enjoys long form improvisation because of the opportunity to be taken on a limitless adventure. As long as they can follow the scene and understand the connection between what the improvisers are creating and their suggestion, audience members can become thoroughly captivated and delighted by long form improv.

What follows in this book are some thoughts on how to better approach long form improvisation, so that it can more successfully reach an audience as a piece of comedy entertainment.

2

APPROACHING LONG FORM

ONE OF THE great challenges of long form improvisation happens before the long form improvisation even begins. It is the name of the kind of improvisation itself.

Long.

Form.

The psychology that occurs before the suggestion is even gathered already greatly affects the way an ensemble approaches the experience. If I could offer one equation that sums up the human mind and its approach to improvisation, it would be this:

The more importance you place on an improvisational experience, the less likely you are to play.

Children don't approach their playtime as "important." It is actually quite the opposite, which allows the freedom to "let go" and play. With adults and improvisation, it is the same thing. If improvisers approach the improv experience feeling as though the stakes are high, then they are more likely to create safeties and guarded behaviors in order to protect themselves in that "important" experience. They may travel through scenarios and outcomes in their head beforehand in order to thoroughly evaluate the situation. These improvisers feel they have to keep themselves from being slow and boring, and suddenly they are building walls around their ability to be spontaneous and funny. The irony is somewhat apparent. It is THE paradox of improvisation—the "thinking about" vs. the "doing and playing." That which is perceived as "important" helps the thinking part, but limits the "just playing around" part.

The effects of "importance" on improvisation are obvious in many examples, like the way a performer changes his or her approach to the show because there is a producer in the audience, or a parent, or an instructor, or a celebrity, or even an arbiter of the schedule of improv ensembles. Because that particular show has more "importance" associated with it, the mental approach to it shifts. It's no longer "Hey, let's just play around. Who cares? Have fun!" It's "Hey, we have to do a good job because there is a television producer and an agent in the house tonight." That shift creates a more guarded mindset for the performers and can—and often does—greatly affect the degree of play produced in the improvisation. There is a feeling of, "Yeah, we usually just have fun, but tonight is different. Now we have to REALLY have fun in order to create a favorable perception of our abilities as comedic talent, so let's perform all of the necessary steps to adhere to this important context and produce that impression."

I stretch it, but the shift in thinking and the internal monologues that occur among performers aren't far off.

Greater evidence of this is the thousands and thousands of improv auditions I have watched over the years. While facilitating auditions at The Second City, I have noticed—time after time after time—wonderful and playful and funny and great improvisers get stuck in their heads and end up not being entertaining or exciting onstage. The reason for this is the degree of importance that they place on the audition experience. It is VERY IMPORTANT, so their minds treat it as such. They protect themselves with thinking and safe moves and appropriateness and a much more formal demeanor because it is so IMPORTANT to them. Auditions, without even trying, accentuate this feeling simply by virtue of what they are: a wall of human judgment with great stakes attached. "Will these people think I am good enough to get the job?" Improvisers often adhere to this morass of emotion in an audition room, and it renders them as stiff, uninspired thinkers who are unable to play. It breaks my heart to see my many-talented friends fall under this "important" veneer year after year. It's like telling a child, "You better play and have fun and really look like you are having fun, or you will not get lunch money tomorrow. Now look like you are *having fun*! Do it, or else!" Under those conditions, the fun is hard to be had. The child will not eat lunch tomorrow.

I've also noticed that when performers no longer really care—maybe they're a little mad at a place or have created a body of work outside of it or are just plain tired of waiting—their auditions are significantly more funny and playful. More often than not, they get hired after that audition because they have eliminated the idea of importance. The experience doesn't have the same stakes as it once did now that the performers aren't focused solely on the gravity of the situation. They've gotten rid of the feelings and thoughts associated with "I'm really, really doing this, so it better be good," and replaced them with "I don't care. I'm just going to play around with wild abandon." It's the unrestrained, carefree playing around that leads to funny and exciting choices, which often leads to employment.

Anyone reading this might think, "Okay, I'll just fake not caring." Good luck going through all of the mental mechanizations necessary to trick yourself into not caring while the importance secretly still lies underneath. You still have to then try to shirk off those layers to achieve the "abandoned way of thinking" that is necessary to produce a vital, engaging, and funny improv audition. What? Yes. With all this going through your mind, it will take a colossal effort just to topple over the line.

What I mean by "topple over the line" is getting past the imaginary line of fear that separates the player from the playing area. The more importance that is placed on the experience, the more difficult it is to cross this line.

So…

Long.

Form.

So with long form, you're already in a bit of trouble when it comes to the idea of importance. The two words alone suggest nothing else: Long and Form.

Long.

It is long.

Time in improvisation is a remarkable thing. Given that it is one of the most widely used ways of measuring events around us in life, it is no coincidence that we see its constant effect on improvisation. If you want to create a playful state and minimize the feeling of "being in your head" or having great meta-self-judgment about what you are doing while you are doing it, then reduce the length of time you are improvising. The less time you have, the more likely you are to have fun. The less time you have, the less importance you will place on the event, thereby maximizing your chances of playing around without care. Inversely, the longer the amount of time, the greater the chance that you will enter an overly safe and measured state of thinking, minimizing your chances of making courageous and playful choices in an improvisation experience.

If I tell a group of people that we are going to improvise five-second scenes, one after another, the result is always short scenes that are physical, begin their content in the middle of a sentence, and have a wider character and emotional range. The feeling is,

"Who cares? It's just five seconds. It doesn't matter. What could possibly go wrong?" The perception that the experience is extremely important is eliminated because it seems so short that it is indeed disposable. This leaves room for the psychology of purer play. An improviser's carefree side is more readily available to him as a result of not having to form protective thoughts to confront the fear of a longer, more important experience.

The same sense of abandon could happen if I said, "We are going to improvise fifty scenes in twelve minutes." That's around fifteen seconds per scene. Fifty of them in less than fifteen minutes! This creates a fervor of playful improvisation, where people make choices based on right brain instinct with no room for self-judgment. Both the pace and the volume of scenes in a condensed amount of time leaves only enough room for play. "It isn't that important. It's fifty scenes we'll forget about after twelve minutes! What could go wrong? I'm going to just go for it!" The translation of this could be, "Because of the context of maximizing the volume of scenes and minimizing the time in this experience, I am going to improvise in a playful manner." Stoic, but true.

Minimizing time lessens importance, therefore encouraging play.

And...

The opposite is rather true, as well:

You are now going to improvise one scene for five minutes.

Suddenly the psychology shifts. I don't know if you've ever improvised a scene for five minutes, but it is a very long time. Don't let the "five" fool you. Five seconds is easy, but five minutes is a long time, especially for a single scene that is not embedded in a longer show.

The fact that the volume has been decreased to one scene and the time has been lengthened to five minutes changes the way everyone perceives the experience. Suddenly the feeling of how important the improvisation is increases. "I only have one opportunity to do a good scene, and I have to keep it going for a full five minutes." Five minutes no longer feels disposable; it feels "real." The thinking becomes, "Yeah, before we were just playing around doing fifteen-second scenes, but now we are really improvising." This becomes "the one"—the real one—the one that is longer and more substantial and has more weight. This is the important one.

The *long* one.

If there is any doubt, the many improvisation auditions I have run usually call for a bunch of short scenes followed by a longer one. Typically it is an invitation to do a few five-second scenes and then a scene for a minute or a minute and a half. The relative perspective is interesting. In this context, the minute scene is perceived as the longer one, the one that matters, the important one. These "long" scenes are not approached with the same demeanor of play as the short scenes. They are approached a bit more sincerely and measured because they are the "real" one.

Warm-up scenes are similar. At the top of a rehearsal you might hear, "Let's just do a bunch of quick scenes to warm up. Let's just play around and get on our feet with some quick scenes."

The implication that they are just warm-up scenes immediately means that they don't matter. Because of this perception, they are usually playful and performed with abandon and fun. They "get your blood going" and "get your gears turning." They are not real. They are not important. You may even hear, "Let's just do some quick scenes to warm up *before we get started.*" Ah, before we get started with what? Improvising for real? Yes, that's what. We are going to "make up words" in shorter scenes before we get to the real business of why we have gathered today: to "make up words" in real, longer scenes. Actually, it's all just "making up words"— improvising. That definition is a constant. It's the context of time that shifts the perception of importance. *That* is what changes.

And so it goes.

When we approach long form improvisation, we are subconsciously affected by the length of time implied in the name. We often forget the word is there, but it is. This form is "longer" than other kinds of improvisation. It's real, and it's for keeps. We have just been messing around before, but now we are doing long form. It's longer, so let's act accordingly. Let's approach it with the importance its length deserves.

We lose sight of the fact that it's all still just "making up words." Understanding and realizing this psychological shift is a good first step to successfully approaching long form, but it's only half the battle. Now that we can conceptualize the mental obstacles that "long" brings to the table, what about "form"?

Form.

It's long. And it has a form. It has a structure. It has Form. And anything with a form is clearly more important. Things that are shapeless and chaotic and random are less important. These things are fleeting.

Forms are here to stay. Forms are used to pour concrete when you build a foundation.

Forms suggest stability. Forms provide credence to a procedure. You must get all of the forms right for the process to work.

Forms are all business. "Please fill out the correct form and place it in the box." You FORM a thought about how to fill out a FORM in order to FORM a strategy for building a foundation.

> *The line forms on the right.*
> *Is the occasion chaotic and casual and haphazard?*
> *No, it has form.*
> *It is "form"-al.*
> *We will be dressing for the event. It is formal. It is a lengthy, formal event. It is long and formal. It is a Long Form.*

(I will shut up now.)

Let's just say, it is fairly important.

So before you even begin, "Long Form" packs a bit of a subconscious, psychological punch.

> *Ladies and gentlemen, welcome. We are going to be presenting a piece of impromptu improvisation called a long form. The piece will take a single suggestion, and its structure will last for approximately one-half hour. May we have a suggestion of a concept or a theme in order to inspire this piece of improvisation, this longer form of improvisation? Clouds. Thank you. The suggestion will be clouds. (Looks back at the players.) Clouds... let us begin. We will now improvise a long form piece based on your single suggestion of Clouds. Let the humorous improvisation begin. Let us play... (Walks offstage speaking softly.) ...Clouds...*

This is a slight exaggeration of how many long form improvisations are introduced, yet I have actually played after introductions very similar to this one. "Importance" is all over it. The pretension of long form is woven into that introduction. Not only does it not encourage play among the ensemble or team, it also does not provide the context of an improv playground for the audience. Even if the audience doesn't consciously *perceive* the importance in the words, they suddenly *feel* it. The "important" veneer seeps through the performance in many ways, even in the introduction, and affects what is to follow. After the person doing the lead-in walks offstage, softly repeating the suggestion "clouds," you can almost predict what might follow...

A bit of silence. Perhaps an actor coming out and "going to her environment" (creating an imaginary object appropriate to the suggestion). More silence before she looks at her partner and says, "So… Cumulus."

Or perhaps it's a Word Association opening sequence, and after the introduction, a player walks forward, head down, and sincerely utters the word "cumulus." Another walks forward and says, "Heaven." And so it goes.

I will address long form openers with more scrutiny later. I just want you to imagine that first moment as it is being affected by the importance placed on the experience in the introduction. It can create a quagmire that is difficult to penetrate and hard to play within. It often creates a creaky, thoughtful feeling for the group that makes it all the more difficult to break out and have fun.

The term "long form" was coined to not only differentiate the type of improvisation from games, monologues, and short scenes, but to intentionally declare the form on another level of credence and legitimacy. I remember when I first heard about this new Form of Improvisation. It was spoken to me with great reverence, as though a monumental innovation. I was scared of it. It sounded very important. It took me a *long* time to get that it is just "making up words," longer. It is only *important* in that it provides another way to have fun improvising, and having fun improvising is important. But don't lose sight of the very simple fact that it is still just making up words on a stage with friends.

Long form created such a fervor of importance in the world of improvisation that those things everyone was comfortable calling "games," the very foundation of the work of Viola Spolin (the founder of American contemporary improvisation), has now been re-named *short form.*

It's almost as if the thinking went like this:

Their theater does Long Form, an important kind of improvisation. We just do games, but we would like to be respected for what we do. We will say that we no longer

play "games." We will call what we do Short Form. It is
shorter, but it is still a form.

There is great irony in the evolution of that name change. First of all, the creators of the term "short form" were indeed correct. It is all the same. It is merely another "form" or "structure" in which to make up words onstage. It is just shorter. The distinguishing factor of length isn't really what was behind the need to change the name. It was the credibility that accompanies the idea of "form."

The paradox is that many long form and short form theaters and ensembles have dispensed with the word "game" when describing the *structure* for the improvisation they are performing, yet they often speak of and refer to the "game" of, or within, the scene. The importance of *playing* lives on in improvisation, no matter what the event or art form is called.

It's all just improvisation. Making up words on the spot. Remember that, won't you?

3
INTRODUCTIONS

"WHAT'S THIS?" you might ask. "An entire chapter based on introducing long form improvisation?" Yes. As demonstrated in the last chapter, introductions are important. I believe the subject warrants it.

Before getting into introductions, I want to say that "first times" make a huge impression on me. I always take special notice and make sure to never forget them. For example, I will never forget the first time I saw a Second City Mainstage show. I offered the suggestion "cracker salter" as an occupation to be used in their improv set and made the cast laugh. I also won't forget the first time I directed my first day of rehearsal for my first Second City Mainstage show. I remember thinking, "What are all these talented people doing improvising in the afternoon, and how am I the only one lucky enough to be in the room?"

I also watch with special attention when people improvise on the first day of class because that is when they are the most nervous and unfamiliar. Many might just pass this first-day experience as a need to warm up and get comfortable with each other. However, I look at it as a special opportunity to see how the students improvise when they are under pressure, a lot like how they would be in an audition. While directing, I always remember the first impression a scene has on me and on an audience. After repeated versions of a scene in subsequent shows, the comedy wanes for the actors and the director and the producers, so remembering the first impression is useful—if not often vital—to getting the most honest read on the scene. The first time is the only opportunity I will ever have to notice what happens the very first time.

I will never forget the first time I ever saw a long form improvisation. It was the form Harold. I was getting ready to move to Chicago to study improvisation when I was told by a friend about this new thing called long form improvisation. He had already experienced it and said I would love it. By the time I got to Chicago, I was quite excited about it and definitely looked forward to seeing this new type of improvisation. Knowing nothing other than the names "long form" and "Harold," I sat down to see it.

Welcome. We need a suggestion of a theme! Each group tonight will be judged in four different categories and you will be the judge at the end of each group. Each Harold will have games and scenes that come back in time. May we have a suggestion?

Someone offered the suggestion of "money," and off they went. There were about eight people onstage, and they started saying words out loud, one at a time, that were about money. Then there was a scene and another and another and another. Then there was a group scene in the form of a talk show. Then there were more scenes, and some were somewhat related to previous scenes, or some had the same characters as previous scenes, but happened earlier, I think. Then the whole cast *became* money in a series of monologues, saying things like "I am a quarter, do you see me shining?" Then, after that, there was a group song.

Throughout the entire performance, there was a couple in their thirties sitting near me. They didn't laugh. Neither did I. I had no idea what was going on. Not a clue. And the intro didn't help one little bit. I didn't understand what the fuck I was watching. I felt stupid because there was a lot of knowing laughter from other younger people in the audience who clearly knew what was happening. But I didn't. And at this point, after improvising scenes, sketches, and games in college, I felt pretty savvy and educated about improvisation. But I didn't understand. I later found out that a lot of the people laughing were from other groups or teams also performing that night.

Since then, I feel like little has changed in the long form world. I often see people watching long form, then looking at each other and shrugging in confusion or rolling their eyes. And they don't laugh. They look at other people laughing and don't understand what is so funny. They feel like they are supposed to get something, but they just don't. They don't feel like they were invited to the party. They're right, they weren't.

In many contexts, for years and years and then years, there has been an assumption on the part of the theater or the ensemble performing that the audience is savvy about what they are going to see. This is how long form improvisation becomes very insular and "inside." The performers may come onstage and quickly say, "We are going to improvise a long form improv for you now," or "We are going to improvise a succession of unrelated scenes," or they may come out and merely say, "May we have a suggestion of anything, anything at all…" From the performers and the improvisation community's point of view, this almost complete lack of introduction is to demonstrate that not only is there no need for an explanation of the performance that is about to follow, but also to declare that it's an almost obligatory gesture to take a suggestion from the audience, and "anything at all" just further announces their indifference. Sometimes a group will even begin improvising without a suggestion offered, as if to say, "We all know it's really improvised, and we don't have to bother with the inconvenience of getting a suggestion, do we?" My answer would be, yes. Yes, you do. (Unless your name is T.J. Jagodowski or Dave Pasquesi.)

And yes, in most cases, you need to explain what the hell is going on. Otherwise, it becomes a very inside, exclusive, and elitist art form.

I saw this happen very recently at my own theater. A group of students were doing a special class performance, and they had invited friends and family. For their introduction, they said to the audience, "Can we have anything? Give us anything at all." Many audience members were already lost. "Give them anything? Anything what? What is this?" Often some audience members don't even fully understand what improvisation is. If you spent an afternoon at the Second City box office, you would hear time after time, "No, it isn't standup. No, it's more than one performer. It's six actors performing sketch comedy—unrelated scenes and songs, much like you might see on *Saturday Night Live*. And the third act is an improvisation set. Oh, that's where they get a suggestion from the audience and make up the comedy right before your eyes."

Long form improvisation has desired more widespread acceptance for the last twenty-five years, but it still constantly carries the assumption that everyone in the room is "in the know" about what's going on. This tradition continues because out-of-the-loop audience members either never come back, are too scared to speak up for fear of feeling stupid around those who invited them, or don't care enough to pursue it. I have often asked audience members straight-up after a long form show, "Did that make sense to you? Did you understand what was going on?" Far too often, they will pause and then reply, "Honestly, I had no idea. It made no sense at all."

This insular performance context has further been fueled by the very schools and theaters that teach and perform long form.

For some, it has nearly become a part of the business model. It is true that the audience of a long form show is quite often made up mostly of students of improvisation, so they actually DO have a knowledge base and understanding. This usually occurs more during the week, though. Perhaps on a Wednesday night at 9:30, it will be mainly improvisation students and enthusiasts. But at 8:00 on a Saturday night, it's a different group altogether. We all want this kind of audience to see our work in order to gain that greater widespread acceptance, but they may have little understanding of what we are performing.

I am not asking us to pander to each audience with a child-like introduction presented at every show. I'm merely asking people to look around the room, pay attention, and try not to alienate new audience members.

Yes, if it is mainly improvisers, we can tailor our intro to those people. But if it's mainly a commercial audience, we can turn up the heat on the clarity we provide in our introductions. Even in those inside-off-night shows, I'll bet there are still at least two to six people who are new. Everyone deserves a context for the performance that they are about to watch. Everyone deserves to be invited to the party. Everyone deserves to enjoy the product they have come to see. This is the key to moving from just messing around with your friends to more accepted long form improvisation with a wider audience base.

I can assure you that the essential component to gaining audience acceptance is the introduction. An audience will accept so much more if you just have the courage and take the time to actually *explain* it to them.

"Our audiences just don't get it!" My response is, "No, YOU just don't get it. You don't get the value of setting up a proper context and providing audiences with the road map necessary for them to find enjoyment in the show."

For well over a month, the second act of a show that I directed on the Second City Mainstage started with a ten-minute, two-person, improvised relationship scene. We constructed these improvised scenes so that the idea of getting a laugh was discouraged and unimportant, and this made it so that they could not be sold out or joked away. There was a lot of fear in doing something so high-stake and interpersonal in such an important venue.

We found that all we had to do was properly explain what we were doing. Suddenly, the audience was totally on board. Totally on board. Totally.

> *We are going to improvise a little longer, slower scene right now. Tina and Kevin are going to make up a scene based on your suggestion of a relationship, like two cousins. Could we get a suggestion of a relationship? Siblings. Great. Sit back and enjoy this improvised scene based on your suggestion of "Siblings."*

The audience base for that venue is sixty percent tourists, the majority of whom had not seen anything more than *Whose Line is it Anyway?* before that show. But we invited them to the party, and they were fully on board, cheering for the courageous success of the scene. They sat back and enjoyed the experience, and since they did, so did the performers. Because the audience was not alienated, instead treated with respect as intelligent and competent participants, our potentially risky undertaking was a success.

I encourage all of us to remove the pretentiousness of long form improvisation in our approach to the audience. They don't care about anything other than having a good time, and it is our job to provide them with a context in which they can appreciate the performance and laugh along.

Even though it's been twenty-eight years since I first saw long form and had no idea what was going on, the same problem still exists today. Just last night, even at The Annoyance, I saw a montage of unrelated scenes and monologues based on a single suggestion. Many in the audience were clueless as to what was happening. It is laborious and tedious to screech the same monologue over and over in regard to setting up improvisation, I know. But if long form improvisation wants to one day reach its goal of being accessible to a larger audience and enjoying greater commercial success (without radically changing what it intrinsically is), then its context must be properly explained.

I have personally done the introduction for Freeze Tag, a game that ends the improv sets of many successful sketch comedy theaters around the world, at least five hundred times. There is always a large percentage of the audience that has never heard of—let alone seen—Freeze Tag, so someone in the cast must introduce it every time.

Ladies and gentlemen, we are going to improvise one last time this evening. Two actors are going to be doing a scene and at any time one of the other actors may yell "freeze," at which point, that actor will tag out one of the actors and take on his exact body position, and the scene will change entirely. All we need to get started is a suggestion of something that you said today...

Each time I introduce Freeze Tag, I think to myself, "I am going to describe this for the very first time. To the best of my ability, I am going to thoroughly describe what is going to happen so that the audience actually understands it. I don't want to be condescending, but I am going to make it important to myself that I explain it." And I do. And I am proud of the way that I introduce Freeze Tag... now. This pride comes after years of rattling it off at full speed in a haphazard way, and then tacking on a final insult to the audience, "You'll figure it out..."

Imagine if twenty-eight years ago someone had taken the professional and courteous trouble to merely say:

> *Hi, we are going to improvise for you right now. We are going to get a suggestion from you and improvise a lot of scenes based on that single suggestion. As we go, sometimes the scenes will continue where they left off, sometimes there will be brand new scenes, and sometimes group games and monologues will emerge, all inspired by your suggestion.*

Then I would have been invited to participate in the experience, in the know, and I would have enjoyed it a lot more.

If I have sold you on the value of the introduction itself, I now want to sell you on the value of rehearsing introductions. Many, many people don't know how to be themselves in front of an audience. They only know how to perform with the protection of the improv scene, the character, or point of view they are portraying. Being yourself onstage—addressing the audience as *yourself*—is another skill set entirely. It is a facet to your performance that is often ignored or dismissed as a given or as good enough. The ability to portray one's self onstage can either sink or propel performers in improvisation and sketch comedy. It's part of the deal. It's an important element to an evening of improvisation, unlike traditional theatre. If you were acting in a production of *Long Day's Journey into Night*, for example, you probably wouldn't ever have to stand in front of the audience as yourself. Lights up, and the play begins. The only glimpse of "you" that the audience might glean is your reaction to the applause of the curtain call. And that's possibly rehearsed, as well.

With improvisation, though, being yourself is a tangible part of the performance that is all too often taken for granted or not acknowledged.

Rehearse.

Rehearse your introductions to everything. Practice being in front of an audience and introducing a game, a long form, the next group, the next act, or an entire evening. Practice doing outros (the curtain speech at the end of a show or at the end of an evening). Know what you are saying. Know the content inside and out, no matter what it is. Iron out your speech to get rid of filler words and stutters. Package your intros so that they are engaging, present, slick, and fast, yet clear enough to understand. Get them down cold. Be a professional. This aspect of improvisation is far too often overlooked. When executed well, your rehearsed intro creates a truly professional experience, but when disregarded, creates confusion and sets an indifferent tone. Sloppy and unpolished does not equal fun and casual.

Finally, eliminate amateur elements that are the earmarks of an introduction that is unrehearsed:

1. Starting with "How are you guys doing?" The audience is thinking, "I'm doing as well as I was when those other four people asked me that from the stage over the last hour."

2. Saying, "This is going to be fun," or "You're really going to like this." This intro automatically prepares the audience to be judgmental and makes them think, "I'll determine that, thanks," or "It better be." This is also a fear-based move that in essence is saying, "I'm scared. I hope this will be fun."

3. Using filler words, including "uh" and "like." It's hard, but get rid of your "uhs" and stutters. When practicing an intro, try putting a pause where an "uh" is instead. Pauses are a thoughtful, welcome presence in introductions. Filler words are not.

4. Glancing at the floor, off into space, or at the ensemble members onstage. Instead, look at the audience and seek eye contact with individuals as you are doing an introduction. Look at people one at a time and actually explain *to* *them* what is going on. Definitely avoid looking at the other players. This will look weak to the audience, almost as if you are seeking affirmation from your fellow improvisers.

5. Speaking quietly or fidgeting. Be loud and be present with your voice and body. An introduction to anything in improvisation IS a performance. You are performing as yourself in front of an audience.

Practicing your stage persona is essential. You will excel if you do and falter if you don't. It's an important edge to have as a sketch comedy or improvisational performer and is neglected all too often.

Tight, professional, accessible introductions that set the tone invite the audience to the party and entertain them along the way. Proper introductions prepare, excite, and engage the audience for the experience that follows, creating the perfect atmosphere for successful long form improvisation.

Thus, a chapter devoted to the skill of introduction.

4
SUGGESTIONS

THE SUGGESTION YOU take from the audience, or the "get" as some might say, is what the audience offers in order to affect the performance. In long form, a theme is often asked of the audience in order to embrace a wider and more diverse pool of inspiration than, say, a specific location, occupation, or relationship title, which is often sought in shorter improvised scenes or games.

How an improv ensemble handles the audience's suggestion has always been rather interesting to me. Sometimes the suggestion is all but ignored as the players seemingly disregard it as irrelevant, leaving the audience wondering why they offered one in the first place. Other times, the ensemble extrapolates and breaks down the suggestion in all of its incarnations so much that the audience grows weary of the very thing they offered up.

I've seen groups take a suggestion, dance around it, and seemingly never touch upon it. As the ensemble is looking at each other, extending their hands out, and saying, "Whoosh," the audience is wondering what the hell this has to do with their suggestion of "nanoscience." Other times, like with a Word Association, an invocation, or a musical opener, the suggestion is dissected so thoroughly that the audience is thinking, "Okay, I get it. You're listing all the different uses for nanotechnology over and over and breaking apart the syllables. Get on with it already." But instead of moving on, the first scenes following this opener use the same information, and the audience continues to have the offered suggestion pounded back into their brains in extraordinary, list-like, excruciating detail.

I'm going to try to sell you on a strange middle ground between avoidance of an audience suggestion and the pandering, laborious dissection of which I just spoke.

To do this I'll start here:

The audience's need to have their suggestion attended to is immense.

Attended to.

In most improvisational scenarios, it is vital to empower the audience to accept that what they are seeing is entirely made up on the spot. Attending to their suggestion is the only way they can see that this is true. In improvisation-saturated communities and cities, as I mentioned before, it is so easy to forget this need because of the assumption that everyone in the room *knows* the performance is improvised. Even in situations where the audience completely *does* know and believe the show is improvised, if you ask for a suggestion and don't reflect it in the performance, then the audience will be distracted. "Why? Why are they talking about *that?* What does this have to do with our suggestion?" These questions will linger in any audience's mind, whether savvy to improvisation or not, until the suggestion is finally acknowledged. That is why the need to have the suggestion attended to is immense.

Now, notice I am carefully using the words *attended to.* This is done with my next point in mind:

What it takes to satisfy the audience's need for their suggestion to be attended to is minimal.

While the suggestion must be utilized, it doesn't take much for an audience to feel that their suggestion has been incorporated. It doesn't have to be much at all. For example, if the suggestion was "ocean," all one of the actors has to do is say something like "blue and infinite" as they look into the house during a scene, and the audience is satisfied that their suggestion has been *attended* to. The actual scene that follows might be a couple on a cruise ship looking over the rail and talking about their divorce. The ocean setting was hinted, and that is enough for the audience to be extremely open to whatever happens next. Their need for closure in regard to the use of the suggestion has been alleviated. Their left brain, or analytical side, is satisfied, and they are now willing to accept anything. They have been given the respect that their influence upon the improvisation deserves.

Given that, I want to pitch you this:

Once the suggestion has been attended to, the audience will successfully make their own additional connections.

Now that the performers have met the need to have the scene relate to the suggestion, the audience members' analytical brains will continue to connect the dots. They will make their own patterns of recognition in ways that the improvisers can't even imagine and definitely didn't intend.

For example, if in the aforementioned divorce scene one of the players says, "Yeah, I hate to bring this up, I really do…," someone in the audience will think, "Ah, making waves. Clever." If an improviser states, "Well, we've been having trouble for a couple years now," an audience member might think, "Stormy relationship." If one of the actors snaps, "You don't have to bite my head off!" the lady in front imagines, "Shark attack!" I may be too blatant and over the top with my examples, but audience members *do* think this way.

Once the audience has started to make those connections, they will really, really stretch it to find associations and reconcile the improvisation with the theme. Basically, once the ball is rolling, the audience will do all the work for the ensemble. The actors' responsibility in regard to the suggestion is fulfilled, and the audience's need to be hit over the head with their contribution is greatly minimized.

Try this exercise as a group. Have a player sit out and write a theme on a piece of paper. To start with, make it a broad idea or concept, like "transportation." After his suggestion is determined but *not* shared with the group, have the ensemble do a series of improvised scenes with nothing in mind and no need to make any connections between the scenes. Keep them short—say fifteen to thirty seconds apiece. During each one, the player sitting out should make a note every time the scene touches on his chosen theme.

Now you might be thinking, "What? How can the other ensemble members incorporate his theme? They don't even know what it is." Exactly. It's amazing how often he will make a connection between the scenes and his unrevealed suggestion. For example, going off of the theme "transportation," in one scene, perhaps someone took a cab to get there. "Cab" is a type of transportation, and so the actor sitting out will make a note of it. A player might begin the next scene with, "Do you know when the bus is arriving?" Again, a bus is a mode of transportation, so another note will be made. Maybe in the next scene, no connection will be made. Then, in another scene that seems to have nothing at all to do with transportation, a character could mention plans to move in a few days. The observer may think, "Moving will require a moving truck and other modes of transportation to get things from one place to another. A bit of a stretch, but I thought of it, so it's a connection." A scene later an improviser says, "I am reading your thoughts," so the moderator writes down "thought transmission" as a transportation element.

After around twenty to thirty short scenes, have the player read his connections to the suggestion. See if someone in the ensemble can figure out the theme from the list of associations. Try this exercise again with various players coming up with a few other types of secret suggestions. Have the group try to do scenes that are as different as possible from one another to make it hard to find multiple connections with the theme. (Now all of you go get an ice cream cone!)

During this exercise, not every scene will relate to the secret theme, for sure. But you will be amazed by how many do. Regardless of the intentions of the players, connections will be made in the mind of the observer. You may be thinking, "But he *knows* the suggestion, so he is actively *looking* for associations. He will justify the improvisation and conform it to his theme."

Exactly.

That's my point. During an improv show, the audience *knows* the suggestion, so they will do just that. As long as you attend to the theme, the audience will continue to make connections for you where you don't even know they exist, so the burden of consciously linking the improvisation to the suggestion is greatly lessened.

All of this adds up to reveal:

1. Yes, you have to attend to the suggestion the audience gives you.

2. You don't have to kill yourself doing it; just acknowledge it.

3. The audience members will make a lot of connections to the suggested theme on their own.

Am I saying that the ensemble can ignore the suggestion after the opener and the first scene or two? Yes, probably, but I'm not necessarily recommending that. I'm simply saying that the performers don't have to kill themselves, or the audience, by repeatedly hammering the theme home. I've done 4,893 shows where the audience gives a suggestion, it inspires the first few scenes, and then it is pretty much tossed aside. I can't imagine an audience member approaching after a show and saying, "Wow, that was hilarious! You guys blew me away! Uh... ya know... You only used the suggestion for the first four and a half scenes, and then it was only here and there maybe five more times... but still, the funniest improv I've seen in a long time!"

Due to the particular structure of long form, it's important to attend to the theme more lightly throughout than when performing a montage of disparate scenes. The audience grows weary of exploring the same theme over and over and over for a half hour to forty minutes. They don't *know* that they will grow tired of the suggestion when they offer it, but they certainly *learn* it firsthand after the eleventh scene about clouds. Even if the players have taken the theme from "weatherman" to "heaven," it can still grow tiresome. Boring. Repetitive.

To add to this tedious risk, long form training often advises that the opener, beginning scene, or game is a place to discover information that will help us improvise later. So, after getting the suggestion from the audience, we typically use the opener to mine for material for use in the improvisation that follows.

This notion seems so logical that I am almost afraid to say it, but I have always had a bit of a hard time with this idea: "I am entertaining people and inventing in the moment, but I am also creating things to memorize for later in the improvisation."

I know that these words don't travel through an improviser's mind literally, but the feeling is there. It contributes to the actor's perception that the opener is important and has significant purpose, which leaves him with less room to just fuck around and have fun. "I have to think of things to use later, not just have fun and throw away lines now. In order to do that, I have to take note of everything so that these concepts can inspire subsequent scenes." After I have formed an idea for a scene based upon this remembered information, I have to somehow impose the same concept on the improvisation that is happening right now. I have to force it in there without it looking forced in there. And while doing that, I am supposed to stay in the moment, listen to my partner, and have fun, all at the same time.

Isn't this what we are told NOT to do? Pre-think an improv scene? Conceptualize something beforehand and then attempt to have the scene conform to those preconceived beats? We are taught early on in improv training that this type of thinking is futile at best. We are taught that we can't control all the unforeseen variables coming at us from others onstage and that the weighty exposition necessary to force an idea into a scene is contrived, premise-based, and obvious.

You may be thinking, "Well, the information from the opener isn't something that you use to *write* an entire scene, it's just there to *inspire* the scene."

Okay. Then let's look at the word "inspire."

Inspire.

It's a good word, and it's used in improvisation all the time. I use it a lot myself. We use "inspire" instead of "influence" or "affect" because "inspire" carries with it the inference of emotion and passion. In truth, to inspire, influence, or affect something is really just to trigger it. All of these words denote the starting point of a concept, not the actual content of the idea itself.

So if the inspiration is "clouds," then the idea of clouds is simply where the scene begins. The scene must then be open to free improvisation. In reality, when we store an idea away for later use, we are storing an entire concept, not just an inspiration.

Therefore, why not be truly inspired by what is happening in the moment instead of trying to resurrect an earlier concept? It's impossible to be spontaneously inspired by a specific idea from a previous scene. Drawing inspiration from what is currently happening onstage is far more organic. When I find words I am tempted to store away, I need to realize that those words are much more relevant to what is happening in the long form *now* (that's why I thought of them now) than they will be to any scenes that develop later. I can and will be inspired by ideas at any time. I don't need the opener as a crutch.

Unfortunately, once someone has created the product of an idea—the concept that he discovered and memorized in the opener—then he wants to *show* that product of his thinking, even if he has to force it a little. He gets tied down by this one "good" idea, and it limits his ability to process and create in the moment. Instead of getting caught up in saving ideas, I would suggest focusing on being inspired by what is actually happening on the stage right now.

I would love to see the day when an opener is truly only inspired by the suggestion, and the burden of creating lumbering information for later is dismissed. Information would still come and the audience would still make connections, yet the players would be capable of thinking in a much more organic way that actually serves what is happening onstage.

I've been in many a long form where I couldn't even remember what the suggestion was at the end of it. In the best improvisation, we may forget the theme because we are having so much spontaneous fun that our analytical brain isn't preoccupied by it. All the long form shows that I thought were fabulous shared these three traits:

1. I never felt the theme was ignored.

2. The audience was never disappointed that we didn't hammer in the theme.

3. I was able to enjoy the amazing, honest improvisation.

It all works together in concert. And brilliant ensembles aren't burdened by information, but instead allow the suggestion to truly inspire and free them.

The reason I'm giving the suggestion so much emphasis is because people learning long form give it *so much emphasis*, even though, in my observations, it most often just messes them up. As you will read later, I'm actually not averse to thinking ahead in improvisation. In fact, I encourage it. Just not in this content-dependent, expository way.

Getting back to the suggestion... If it is acknowledged and attended to quickly at the top of the show, and then lightly used throughout to *inspire* scenes, it can become another kind of valuable tool: a *through-line*. Instead of belaboring the suggestion, the ensemble could loft it in the air from time to time, creating a free association without judgment or sometimes even conscious thought. To demonstrate this idea, think of the suggestion as ringing a bell. A bell rings any time there is a connection with the theme. In our example of "clouds," a bell rings with the word "fluffy" or "billowy" or "overcast." The bell gently reminds us of the theme. It's not forcing, but lightly asserting. Bells are nice.

Think of a church bell ringing in your neighborhood for a wedding or Sunday morning church. It is used at certain times to announce different occasions. However, if the bell rings relentlessly over and over, especially in the same rhythm, it loses all meaning and becomes, well, just plain annoying. Like this bell, the suggested theme rung over and over again in a long form will lose its impact and most likely become obnoxious.

It's a savvy ensemble that can lightly place the theme here and there, as if ringing a lovely bell. This is the group that uses the suggestion as a tool to inspire and lift the energy of the show while creating beautiful connectivity throughout.

5

OPENERS

AN OPENER FOR long form improvisation is simply the first thing the audience sees. It is what starts the long form experience after the audience offers what is usually a single suggestion.

Common openers include:

- Monologues

- Songs

- Long Scenes

- Environment Explorations

- Word Associations

- Group Scenes

- Invocations

- Movie Trailers

- Narrations

- Two-Person Scenes

- Interpretive Dance

These openers can be chosen ahead of time and rehearsed, or they can be as organic and original as the scenic improvisation that is to follow. Either approach is fine. Neither is necessarily better; they are just different.

Descriptions of the above long form openers are an easy search on the amazing Internet, so I won't list each one's attributes. Instead, I wish to explore the approach, thinking, and execution of any long form opener. I will, however, use a couple of the abovementioned openers as examples to illustrate different facets of long form openers.

So.

The first step to improvising a good opener in long form is to decide that you are actually doing a show in front of an audience.

"What's that?" you say.

I said, you must, as an ensemble, agree that you are creating a piece of entertainment for an audience and that the launch of the show is more important than your need to warm up.

You must decide and accept this *first.*

"Well, of course we are doing a show," you say. "Of course we know that!"

All. Too often. We forget that.

We often forget that we are actually doing a piece of comedy *entertainment* because we are so immersed in the *work* of doing a long form. Add to this the fears that come with any improvisation, the constant encouragement to play "slower" and "to the top of your intelligence" in long form, and the need to mine the openers for ideas to use later on, and you can end up with a very cautious, anti-playful experience for both the players and the audience. This, from my observations, is when long form gets into a bit of a measured, thinky mentality. We completely forget to have fun.

Have. Fun. Indeed.

With all the pressures on us, it's not surprising that we actually do forget that we are creating a show. All of this is the recipe for a room filled with pretension, importance, and fear. It's the reason that at the top of many long form improvisations, pace, presence, theatricality, and performance take a backseat. It's why a lot of openers begin slowly, with pauses between words and players with their heads down in the back line and even onstage. It's the reason that a lot of openers are, well, boring.

Let's look at the worst culprit from our list of openers above: Word Association. In this opener, the ensemble is given a suggestion, and then the players usually walk around onstage randomly and intermittently say words that the suggestion reminds them of or that they "associate" with the suggestion. Word association, just like in therapy.

So if the audience's suggestion is "justice," the group would begin walking around stage until someone, rather serious-sounding, says, "Scales." A few seconds pass, and another player might say, "Blind." A few more seconds pass, and someone, looking down at the stage, says, "Law." And then another player immediately jumps in with, "And order." There is a slight murmur of response from the audience because of the faint reference recognition. Then one player stops walking, holds his arms out, and says, "Lady Justice." Another player steps forward after a second, crosses his arms in front of his chest, and shouts, "League of Justice." In a craggy character voice, a player jumps in with "Judge Judy." The audience kind of laughs at this reference, and a player calls, "Here comes da judge!" More seconds pass. Another player, head down and walking, mutters, "Poetic justice." A player then shouts, "We must get poetic justice!" Another player stops and also shouts, "We must have poetic justice!" And a third player, "Give us poetic justice!" The rest of the players now start shouting, "Give us poetic justice!

Give us poetic justice!" with a lot of energy and volume, over and over.

At this point, the audience is smiling a bit and watching thoughtfully, but what they are most likely thinking is, "What the fuck is going on?"

It's a good question. What *is* going on?

They may also be thinking, "Have they started? Is this the show? Or are they just warming up?"

Has the piece of comedy entertainment begun, or is the ensemble doing a warm-up for the comedy entertainment that will start in a bit?

Long form suggests that the answer is both. The opener helps the group think about and break down the suggested theme for future use, and it also serves as a beginning to the experience the audience is watching. The idea of long form might imply that it's even okay that the audience is a bit confused, because the opener is meant to help the actors find their way organically.

The idea of an opener for long form improvisation looks absolutely fabulous on paper. The opener takes a theme and allows the players to start dissecting it in order to inspire and empower the improvisation that will follow. It sounds great.

In theory.

In practice, however, as I mentioned earlier, thinking with the goal of creating and remembering words or concepts inhibits the playful sense of fun.

But what else is happening in this opener? Players are taking pauses, walking around at random, heads often looking down, thinking about stuff. Occasionally they say words with a fair amount of weight and importance behind them. The ensemble is clearly only thinking about words that remind them of other words to say. And they are thinking that if they can get a laugh off a reference or a break in this feeling of important tension, all the better. What they are not thinking is, "I am performing a show, and I want to create pace, excitement, play, presence, and theatricality." Nope. To the audience, they are just walking at random with their heads down.

Can you tell how I feel about the Word Association opener? I like it, *in theory*. I just don't care for what it does to the audience at the beginning of a fun night of improv. When I watch improvisation, I don't want to watch the performers think about what they will do, or dissect what arsenal of information they may or may not utilize in the performance that follows. No, I want to be invited to the fun right away. I want the *performance* to begin.

And while this opener does look like it is good for the ensemble since it *is* providing a foundation of information, it is also doing psychological performance damage by heightening the idea of the importance of the experience, thereby making it less likely that the ensemble will break out and just play.

Every opener not only launches the show but also declares what the show will be. Often, and I do mean often, openers like Word Association declare a show to be slow, disconnected from the audience, filled with measured thinking, void of character or point of view, bloated with pauses, and rather lacking in laughs. Very rarely will a show be able to break away from the tone, whether engaging or just plain boring, that is set by the opener.

But what would happen to the entire show if the "justice" Word Association opener detailed above proceeded more like this?

The split second the person doing the intro repeats the suggestion "justice," a player launches downstage left. He freezes with his arms spread open as if holding scales and says, "The scales of justice." Another player gets immediately behind the first player, puts his hands over his eyes, and says, "Justice is blind." While both of these players hold their poses, another player shoots downstage right, puts a hand above his eyes as if looking a great distance, and says, "The Halls of Justice." With NO time passing, another player gets behind the player at stage right, puts his fist in the air and shouts, "The League of Justice." These two players hold their poses like the first.

Now a fifth player travels down center, between the frozen pairs, and says in that craggy voice, "I'm Judge Judy. What did you think you were doing?" This player also freezes, and a sixth player comes behind her, points out toward the audience, and shouts, "You're out of order!" Everyone in the three frozen pairs now shout, "No, you're out of order!"

They then break out of their frozen positions, begin to move around the space, and repeat, "No, you are out of order!" while pointing at each other. This builds in volume until a player shoots downstage, points at the audience, and, in an accusatory tone, says to them, "No! You are all out of order!" Without a pause, another player comes downstage to join that player in a line, points to the audience, and says, "You are." Another player joins with "Out!" The fourth, fifth, and sixth player join in a now-distinct line. The fourth player says, "You are out," the fifth says, "You are out!" and the sixth says, "You are out," and then suddenly whispers while dropping his hand, "You are out of order..." He then turns toward a player at center stage without missing a beat and, in a stern, loud voice, says, "You're representing me, not them." The player at center immediately responds, "I am your attorney, and I am telling you not to testify." The other players slowly, yet with purpose, travel upstage away from the two-player scene that has organically developed from the opener. There is a weighty pause before the third line of dialogue officially begins the first scene of this particular long form.

This example of an opener was completely, spontaneously made up. You might assume that it had been choreographed beforehand, and while that isn't a bad thing (I'll discuss this further below), something this clean and yet engaging can come organically from a group playing with four things in mind:

1. Extract and associate information from the audience's suggestion.

2. Recognize and accept organic patterns.

3. Acknowledge that the rhythm established in the opener will affect the entire piece.

4. *Perform* the opener for an audience that wishes to be entertained.

Basically, attend to the audience suggestion, create a pattern, declare the pace, and do it with performance energy.

The opener that I just outlined retained the desired benefit of breaking down the suggestion and forming associations just as the first, slower version did. The key is that just doing that is not good enough. The players in the second version kept theatricality and performance in mind, knowing that all of this can be achieved at the same time.

While it is obvious that I am not a fan of mining information from an opener to be used in the subsequent scenes, some forms, by virtue of their rules, insist that you have to. Even in these forms, declaring a theatrical launch for the show is the ultimate goal.

How does an ensemble achieve this type of opener? The first step is structure. It could be that a group does indeed choreograph their opener, and bless them if they do. Many are choreographed, and I am all for it. Oftentimes the alleviation of the burden of creating structure in improvisation by applying choreography will give greater freedom for creating fun content.

Set choreography is not always necessary, however, to create an opener with structure. In the example above, each player merely had to recognize the natural staging patterns the other players were creating. Pattern recognition, while math-ish (but fun math), is a key component of any improv. Actively using it in the opener, in my opinion, is better because it encourages vitality, spontaneity, and fearlessness. It launches the show by getting the performers "out of their heads."

In my example particularly, players three and four simply chose to create a staging pattern by mirroring the staging of the first two players. They also continued the content and presentation patterns initiated by the first two players by making points about justice directed out to the audience. All players four and five had to do was continue the patterns already firmly established by the other players.

More specifically, player one created Justice's scales along with a definitive physical choice. Player two then covered his eyes and stated "Justice is blind," thereby declaring the pattern of making a physical choice related to justice while speaking to clarify that physical choice. Player two also created a new pattern by choosing to stand directly behind player one. Based on the new pattern, player three could have chosen to stand behind player two, but instead, he chose to travel to the other side of the stage, providing a more interesting stage pattern for the audience and a larger variety of pattern choices for the remaining players. Player three does, however, keep the first pattern intact by speaking about justice with a solid physical choice. Player four now recognized the two staging patterns formed by the earlier players and chooses to meld them by both following player three to the other side of the stage while also placing herself behind him, etc.

While this is tedious to explain (sorry), the result the audience sees onstage is anything but tedious. They are seeing an ensemble create a theatrical presentation by recognizing what is happening in the moment onstage. Add to that the performers' desire to not let any time go by between lines of dialogue, and you have a group that wants to get the job of extrapolating information and launching a comedic stage performance at the same time done, and done well.

Creating structure through patterns is not something you "find" or "discover" in the opener but is instead an active choice. A player creates something by initiating a move, and then the other players choose to establish it as a pattern through repetition. It doesn't magically appear. It is executed from conscious choice. The opener's build is organically created by the patterns declared as it develops, not tacked on to create a false end to the opener.

Now, without pause and with great conviction, this ensemble has taken simple Word Association and garnered information while executing an entertaining and vibrant piece of theatre. They have also established early on that their long form presentation will have great pace and variety. These concepts have a much greater chance to thrive throughout the entire long form experience as a result of the improvisers' strong declaration right off the bat. While it's hard to manufacture fearless, vibrant fun out of deep, slow thinking, it's also hard to kill positive energy after it has been firmly established.

So.

The second step in achieving a proactive and engaging opener is momentum. I'm going to illustrate this concept using a simple environment exploration opener. An environment exploration is simply building a physical scene based on the suggestion. This could or could not be accompanied by Word Associations or other types of openers, as well. The audience provides a theme, and one by one, the players commit to forming a related scene by miming activities that would happen in that environment. I have seen this opener executed in many different ways, some with the audience falling asleep, and others with an active and engaged audience. *How* an environment exploration is executed makes the difference between the funs and the doldrums.

Between play and tedium.

For example, let's say the host, or person doing the intro for the show, gets the suggestion of "bank." It's shouted first by the audience member making the suggestion, repeated out loud by the host, and then softly said by the players a couple of times in a contemplative way. After that, there is a three-second silence while the suggestion is "considered" by the ensemble. Not so suddenly, one player starts to travel very… slowly… downstage, gets to an area that in their mind is a bank station, reaches for a pen, and starts to write out a deposit slip or a check. This player has finally toppled over the line after some thoughtful silence and consideration of the theme.

After the first person creates the pattern of performing bank business, a second or two goes by before another serious-looking player becomes a bank teller by standing in a sideways profile position onstage. A third player notices the bank-teller choice and approaches the teller as a customer. The teller looks at the person at the bank station and back at the customer in silence, and another second goes by. A fourth player slowly starts walking downstage right, checks a gun, looks around suspiciously, and takes an authoritative stance as the security guard. The guard looks at the person doing business at the bank station, nods, and smiles. The person at the bank station nods back, smiles, and then continues writing. A fifth player now gets in line for the teller as another customer. The sixth player quietly creeps over the line, and looking at something in their hand, becomes another customer in the teller line. The two new customers smile at each other, and then one looks away, waiting. Everyone now looks around in silence for a bit, and then finally transition into something with talking, like monologues, scenes, associations, or whatever.

All in all, a fair amount of time has passed. I just recreated what I described above in my living room twice. The first time took forty-five seconds, so I thought to myself, "Ah, you're going too slow because you're getting ready to make a point about time. Do it again and go faster." And I did. The second time, I felt I was rushing it while still trying to get in everything I described. It still lasted thirty-seven seconds. Over half a minute setting the scene in silence. You may think, "Thirty-seven seconds isn't so long!" Well, it is. Time thirty-seven seconds right now and just sit there in silence. It's a decent amount of time. An adequate amount of time to feel the *importance* and *gravity* of an opening performed in silence. A minute is a long time in improv land. Thirty-seven seconds is an excruciating amount of silence.

If this opener was to lead into a scene, then the words that would come out of this type of opener would be expository exchanges between people who don't know each other, or would suggest small talk or beginning ideas. Things like "Nice day," "Next in line please," "Do you have a deposit slip?" or "How long is the bank open today?" are all slow starters. It's hard to jump straight into high stakes with high energy after beginning with thirty-seven seconds of silence. There is a certain timbre and feel to silence that doesn't invite a sudden burst of energy or the immediate creation of high stakes. There are only so many types of words that thirty-seven seconds of silence invites, and they are the kind of words that subtly break silent tension between humans. "Well, this is certainly a nice bank, isn't it?" or the amazing, "You don't see as many tellers these days, do you?" or the riveting theatrical event, "Have you been in line long?" If this is the opener, then as I said earlier, we will more or less stay slow and silent and cautious and filled with innocuous expository words for the remainder of the show.

What is lacking is momentum. Believe it or not, improvisers could achieve the exact same results in the bank example above— silently setting the scene of different functions in a bank—in about a fourth the time, if that. A group could set this scene in nine seconds, as a matter of fact. The psychological difference between thirty-seven and nine seconds is one of the biggest dilemmas of improvisation: think first and then do, or just do first and then trust that the thinking will catch up.

In the bank scenario, there is a hell of a lot of thinking going on before someone acts. Players don't realize it, but while they are thinking intently in an opener or a scene, time is going by. The audience is seeing people on a stage thinking about what they are doing and *then* watching them cautiously do it.

It creates not only a slow start for the audience, but also a psychological declaration for the players that thinking is more important than playing. This approach allows the idea of importance to creep into their thoughts as well. I say "creep" because it does. It creeps in and is creaky. It produces a sense of thick air that often feels icky and like you will creak as you walk through it, as if cautiously walking through an old house. Creepy and creaky and scared and measured and slow.

Momentum.

I mentioned that the ensemble could create the same thing in nine seconds. I meant five seconds. Now, how does an ensemble create this opener in five seconds? With a little bit of courage, some doing before thinking, and a decent amount of "fuck it" mentality. The group must be fueled by the desire to launch—yes, *launch*—the performance instead of making the audience watch them think their way through the opener in a safe, measured manner. Part of launching is recognizing that doing something—anything—is far more important in improv than what you do. That you move into a position in the bank NOW is far more vital to the energy and excitement of the opener than what you are going to do once you get there.

You may be thinking, "But how do I know what I'm going to be/do until I think about it?"

Two answers:

First, trust. You have to trust yourself. It's like playing Freeze Tag without having a solid idea in your head when you yell, "Freeze!" Trust that if you yell "freeze" confidently as if you do have a great idea, your brain will catch up, and you *will* produce an idea that is just as good as the one you thought about earlier but missed because the body position shifted too fast.

In the "bank" opener, you immediately choose to travel downstage right, not because you know exactly what you're going to do once you get there, but because at that moment the most important thing is to set the *energy* of the opener that is *launching* a long form *entertainment* experience for the audience. To achieve this, you have to put aside your desire to safely construct the idea of a "security guard who is checking his gun," and instead merely move because someone needs to *move*. Your brain can catch up a half second later. What if you move, reach out and grab an imaginary object, discover as it's coming back that it's a gun, and then form the thought that you're a security guard? All of this may seem to happen a bit backwards, but the arrival at the silent initiation of "security guard" is still achieved. The beauty is that it is achieved in half a second as opposed to four, and the audience doesn't have to tally up the time of watching a player think cautiously and importantly and then creep into the scene. But what if you make the move, get there, reach your hand out to grab an object, and it's not a gun? You don't know what it is! Is it a clipboard? Or a Post-it? Uh-oh. If you have a clipboard, are you a manager? What if it were a box? Are you packing your desk up? Oh, my God…

Who cares?

You have to trust yourself. Believe you me, you *will* in that half second simultaneously make a move to a position, reach out, and immediately mentally associate an object to the setting and create a fully functional position appropriate to a bank.

Second answer—and this may surprise you—you have to think ahead and then execute, but do it much faster. "What? I thought you just said not to think!" What I really said is don't take *time* to think. We can't actually stop thinking. Whenever we hear a suggestion like "bank," there is an immediate thought that comes to mind. We can't help it. True word association is an automatic instinct we all have. So when we hear the word "bank," most of us would immediately think "teller" or "security guard" or "bank manager." Oddly enough, it isn't the "thinking of something" that takes so much time in an opener like this, since we almost instantaneously have a thought. It's considering the suggestion, judging our thought to decide if it's the "best" or "right," and then determining a plan of execution that takes our thinking time. If our initial association was "security guard" and we acted upon that immediate thought, we'd be out of the line and into position in the bank in half a second. But we often take a couple of extra seconds to think, "Is that the right choice? Is anyone else a security guard? What should I do? I'll grab a gun... Oh no, will they think I'm a robber? Here I go... Is this a good choice? Here I go... okay." That not only takes a bit more time, but puts the improviser into that cautious, questioning mode of thinking. So, the second answer is to act immediately on the association that comes to mind, because that's how the energy and the momentum of the opener is best served. You think "security guard" and just *go*. This doesn't mean you have to run. As a matter of fact, you could travel very slowly. It means that you "snap" and make a move, which is so vital to your audience and more importantly to your psyche.

Now that I have constructed a model for keeping the momentum up in a silent occurrence—an opener that just sets a scene—these same principles can also be used to benefit openers with words, and *even more so*! Most of the time, it's the words that get us in our head, or get us thinking in a judgmental, left-brain way. We aren't afraid that the audience won't believe our environment; we are ultimately frightened about whether we will be perceived as intelligent or funny or interesting. That's what gets us thinking in that ironic, destructive, self-sabotaging way. So with words, it is the same thing: just get them out there.

Whenever using words in an opener, it's important to get them started as soon as possible, especially for new long form ensembles.

There are times when it is okay to choose as an ensemble to notice and utilize the pattern declaration of *not* talking yet, but with most long form ensembles, particularly the novice ones, their lack of talking right away is guided by individual human fear, not by an individual-becomes-group powerful choice. So when using words in an opener like the bank setting used above, I would advocate the use of words in concert with the establishment of the physical character. Once you're in position, simply use a word you just thought of as you were traveling to that position. For example, the bank teller could cross to his position and say, "Next customer," immediately upon arrival. The ultimate idea is to produce strong momentum right off the bat that will then propel the remainder of the performance.

With trust and the willingness to jump into action instead of taking time to think, improvisers will be able to create and maintain the momentum essential to giving the audience a truly entertaining experience. These actions are actually skills that must be practiced in order for them to be used correctly. Many players, especially those at the beginning of their improv journey, don't normally use "going to and building their environment" as a healthy, powerful tool that makes them more vital and present. Instead, the majority of improvisers use this type of work as time to start thinking some "wicked" thoughts—thoughts that ultimately render them almost immobile.

> *What was the theme, what am I doing, should I say something? I didn't say anything… This isn't funny, what do I do, what is Jenny doing? Is she a teller, should I say something? No one is saying anything. This is slow, I should do something. Is this working? What is Sam doing… is he the manager? What are we doing? Okay, I'm going to say something, but I didn't…*

Everyone is thinking that kind of thing, and by the time a word comes out, it's very cautious and measured. That thinking becomes the tone of the opener. This certainly isn't the theatrical launch to which I referred.

A more experienced player who has developed trust and gumption uses this activity instead as a time to clear his mind and focus on the present. Posing as a security guard, all these players think while cleaning their gun is "clean chamber… look down barrel… make sure safety is on…" Any words eventually spoken by a player this present and in the moment will always come from a powerful, vibrant space.

While building trust, it is important to remember that the thing you think of so carefully beforehand is no better or smarter or funnier than the thing you came up with because you just started talking and trusted that your brain would catch up. In order to truly believe this, try playing a few rounds of Freeze Tag with your eyes closed. It's incredible what your brain will come up with on the spot when it has no other options.

While jumping into words is important, an Invocation opener is all about words, not actions, and yet it's another great example of an opener that almost always lacks momentum. The players say thoughts that the suggestion "invokes" in the terms of "It," "You," "Thou," and "I." For example, using the bank suggestion, the players would say things like "*It* is a building where people keep money," "*You* keep my future safe," "*Thou* art the foundation of our economy!" and "*I* am disappearing into a digital world."

The main difficulty with this opener is that it has importance built in. (It uses the word "thou," for God's sake!) The very nature of this opener invites players to give immense weight to the moment, with great pauses between important-looking people saying important-sounding words. What does this do to the fun and whimsy and play? How does this declare to an audience that the momentum is going to be surprising and theatrical, with laughs and turns and exciting choices? Again, the key to achieving the ideal momentum is to topple over the line and just get the words out there. Get the fear of saying the words out of the way. Once you break through that moment, you are able to get out of your head and create the freedom that you seek in improvisation. After the hundreds of slow Invocation openers I've seen, it would be *so* refreshing to see an Invocation performed in this way:

Thou art an interesting invocation opener.

Now you may be thinking, "Yeah, I hear you. But I've seen a lot of groups do a lot of slow, smart openers with a kick-ass thirty-five minutes to follow." True. Remember, though, that I said that an opener with silence is fine and can be just as theatrical as long as it is approached correctly. I advocate anything that has a recognized organic powerful pattern, even if the pattern is simply traveling slowly to a position and waiting seven seconds in the created environment before we start Scene Painting (describing the environment with a collective point of view). I admire any group that can recognize when silence IS the pattern and go with it. As long as the silence isn't a dangerous think-filled space, it can be powerful.

Huh?

The key words here are: *Recognized. Organic. Powerful. Pattern.*

A group with this approach has practiced being unafraid of silence, and as a result are quite comfortable in it. They are not freaking out. They are present but relaxed and observant and thinking in a very harmonious right/left brain way.

Most beginning improvisation ensembles are not. They are freaking out.

So in the beginning, I *do* advocate getting the words out quickly. One of the dangers of having role models in long form improvisation is that they are usually groups that have worked together long enough and are confident enough to make a slower choice. They are fine just "being" with a physical choice in silence, and they start the first scene after the opener out of choice and power. Beginning long form groups try to emulate the slow build and the important, smart-looking pace of a more experienced ensemble, but possess none of the vital present thinking or trust. They have instead created a slow mess that will haunt them for the duration of the long form, or about a half hour, which seems like two and a half hours in the audience's mind.

Whether the opener is planned ahead of time (like an Interpretive Dance, Invocation, or Word Association), or whether it is created in the moment through the creation and recognition of organic declarations and patterns is irrelevant in the world of theatricality, presence, excitement, and launch. My strong suggestion to any group, particularly a new group, is to learn and rehearse a lot of known long form openers. Make it a point to play with them in many different ways.

Here's an exercise to help!

EXERCISE

Speed through your openers so that you are improvising the lines much too quickly and there are no pauses between words and/or sentences. If you are creating an environment, speak simultaneously with the physical creation. If it's a song opener, sing right a-fucking-way. Dive into these openers with no regard to *what* you are saying. In the beginning, the entire importance should be *that* you say and very quickly. The main goal is to eliminate all time lulls on purpose.

Freeze Tag is a good exercise to use to get to this goal. Either do it blind or at least very fast. I like to encourage the group to just be aware of the *beat* being satisfied, not what *you* are thinking or waiting for. As soon as the beat of what is occurring in the playing area is satisfied or complete, another player should jump straight in. The focus isn't on what she has planned, but on the fact that the scene in progress is complete, and so it's time to move on. She should yell "Freeze!" with excitement as if she has the greatest idea in the world and then run out there and tag out quickly. *Then* she can think of what she is going to say. She should let her mind catch up to her robust commitment, not the other way around. This is the energy that should be poured into every opener. No pauses at all!

EXERCISE

After the ensemble has a grasp on the fast-paced rehearsals, practice your openers again with pauses *and* silence. Create the choice of silence to build an environment. Create an Invocation where there is a three-second silent count before the next "Thou art..." or "I am..." and a good amount of silent space before the divisions of the Invocation. Have silence be a concerted *choice*, not a consequence of thinking and fear. Practice being silent. Practice launching out of silence with power, not trepidation. With such practice, openers can have slow builds without the players being freaked out by the pace or silence. They will be filled with confidence and intent and purpose instead, and the audience won't be wondering when the performers are going to "start to do something."

Dammit.

6
THE BACK LINE

IN MANY LONG forms, there is a back line—a line of players that are positioned onstage, ready to participate, waiting to
do the next scene, or providing ambient or operative sounds or
movements. The back line is usually against a back stage wall or on
the sides.

"Okay," you may say, "and you are devoting an entire chapter
to this idea?"

Yes. There are even some long form improvisation styles that
don't have a back line. This seems like a rather obvious concept
and easy to comprehend, so what is there to write about?

A lot.

I have spent a lot of time observing people performing onstage,
and I have spent a lot of time observing and thinking about what
happens backstage, on the side, and in a back line.

I would love for you to start thinking of the back line in long
form as an entity in and of itself. Whether it's off to the side or
directly onstage, for the purposes of most of this discussion and

the related behaviors and psychologies, I will refer to it as the "back line."

The back line is actually part of the performance. Some people never watch a back line when they are teaching or directing improvisation. For me, however, the back line tells a lot, not only about what is happening in the scenes, but also about the way the show is going and the thinking of the individuals within it.

Before I elaborate on these details about the back line, I would first like to make a pitch for this: do not have one. Many long forms do not have a back line visible to the audience onstage or to the sides.

The primary advantage of not having a back line is theatricality. The absence of a line of actors or improvisers onstage watching or waiting to do anything raises the level of theatricality, the level of the suspension of disbelief. Like it or not, the back line always reminds the audience that they are, indeed, watching improvisation. With a back line, we are watching a group of people watching a group of people improvise, so there is a constant reminder throughout the piece that this is improv. If you remove the watchers on the stage, the presentation grows nearer to what the audience perceives as a more traditional theatrical presentation. The work onstage suddenly has more credence in the eyes of the audience. It's hard to create suspension of disbelief if the very production you are watching doesn't ask you to. Add to this the often casual demeanor of the back line of improvisers—arms crossed, leaning against walls, some sitting down, some looking up, some looking down, some looking at the scene, and some even looking at the rafters or the audience—and you have a collection of focus shifts and behaviors that can quickly distract the audience from the action taking place onstage. It may leave the audience thinking, "If the people in the show aren't giving this that much regard, why should I?" No back line, no distraction nor constant reminder.

As I mentioned earlier, I once directed a Second City Mainstage show where the second act started with a two-person improvised relationship scene. The cast members would rotate the opportunity to perform this scene. I say "opportunity" with enthusiasm. It is a joy to improvise a set two-person scene in this environment. The top of the second act is a golden spot, as the audience members have just relaxed with intermission and are quite willing to now sit back and enjoy something with a little more weight and a slower pace. It's an ideal spot for that type of scene: two actors, two chairs, a suggestion, and seven minutes of improvisation not played for laughs. In our performance, it was the type of theatricality one would have seen in a Nichols and May performance. Both actors dressed in show clothes, perhaps a dress and suit, they really dove into the arc of a relationship-based scene. The audience was right there with them the whole time. The scene was never played for laughs but always got several, and the quality of the laughs was more organic, filtered through the strong familiar past of the characters and the stakes they created with their substantive points of view.

Now imagine placing the other actors onstage watching this. Imagine how it changes the room, the sensibility, and the timbre of the improvisation. The audience sees the other actors as non-participatory observers, like themselves. It's impossible for the audience to not notice them, and with each little glance or shift they make, a trifle of focus is diverted from the scene. It is a different experience than watching an intimate scene focused on only two people. The show is announcing that it would like you to be constantly aware that it is a show, not allowing you to be absorbed completely into the illusion of the drama at hand. The absolute suspension of disbelief that theatre strives for is undermined entirely. Not necessarily a better or worse experience, just different.

Successful two-person improvisational long forms, like *TJ and Dave*, *Messing with a Friend*, or Andy Eninger's *Sybil*, benefit greatly from the theatrical elevation that comes when the players occupy the stage alone. The improvisation itself is the thing—the only thing—on the stage. There are no casual reminders of the improvisation created by the presence of observers onstage along with the two players.

With a larger group improv, however, it is often difficult to achieve a performance without a back line for purely logistical reasons. Besides the fact that the performance may take place in a theater that doesn't have a backstage area, without a back line, the ensemble is unable to hear or see what is going on onstage, there is uncertainty about entering, or players may find it difficult to add to a scene or provide ambience with sound, movement, or narration. In addition, chairs, doors, and other people are collisions waiting to happen, and you never know how many people will be in the next scene. Despite all of these concerns, when the lights come up and there are but three people onstage, there is an elevated feeling of singular focus and theatricality: the actors and the empty stage, not the actors and the empty stage and the other actors. It creates a different kind of improvisational experience.

Add to the performance an audience that is uneducated in improvisation, and we find ourselves with spectators who don't understand why the other actors are onstage in the first place. We so often forget that a back line is something unique to improv and may seem odd and different to virgin audiences. For them, they are here to see theatre. In the last production of *A Christmas Carol* that they saw, the other actors weren't hanging out onstage watching and occasionally making ghost sounds. Any time additional characters are onstage in traditional theatre, it changes the context of the production, and the shifted perception is attended to with great care. In long form, we give it little regard or forget about it entirely.

"Why are those people standing there watching those other people? Are they part of the comedy?" Viewers don't know, and we probably didn't tell them much in our introductions. As I mentioned earlier, "first times" make a mark on me, and the first time I saw long form, I wondered what the rest of the cast was doing onstage. Granted, it took me one minute to get and accept the convention, but I just didn't know the context of long form when I saw it *for the first time*.

So maybe at this point you can accept that *not* having a back line is indeed at least a thing to consider in an improv show, and that it possibly elevates or at least changes the perception of the improvisational experience. But what does it do to the quality of the *comedy*?

When you remove the back line, the tone of the comedy is heightened. The experience suddenly opens up to allow the audience's suspension of disbelief, which allows for infinite possibilities. As I've explained, when the other actors are watching, looking, laughing, shifting, averting eyes, and waiting, the experience can never transcend that convention. While this isn't bad for comedy, just different, I will suggest that it is more limiting. The credence that lone actors onstage gain immediately makes the audience more focused and more willing to penetrate into the relationship of the scene. Without the back line, the possibilities for long form open up greatly, enhancing both the improvisational experience *and* the comedy.

As a side note, I've noticed that whenever "production quality" or "theatricality" enters the world of improvisation or sketch comedy, people begin to fear that the comedy will suffer. The Second City was white walls and bright lights for thirty years. And it worked. When set design and lighting design and color harmony was introduced, there was a fear that the laughs would suffer. They never did. Recently, Matt Hoyde directed a Mainstage show that had a state-of-the art projection system with moving scenic backgrounds that were beautiful. It was a different context, but it gained immediate acceptance from the audience and had the same amount of laughs as always.

An audience will adjust to whatever context you provide for them and still laugh within that context. If the comedy is done well, the audience can enjoy it in any declared context that is true to itself. Whether it's a beautiful production of *A Midsummer Night's Dream* staged at the Shakespeare Repertory Theater or the "Bucket of Yuks Short Form Jam" at Jerry's Tavern, the audience will adhere to that convention if provided enough context for what they are watching.

But let's get back to the thought of not having a back line onstage. You're probably still wondering, "Yeah, but what about all of those logistical concerns you yourself brought up?"

Well, the first solution is for the players to listen as if they were in a back line. This is a simple solution, but not so easily done because we are so prone to talking backstage once we are there. So the very first step in knowing what is going on onstage is to shut the fuck up and actually listen.

The second easy solution is to create hidden sight lines. Most stages already have hidden sight lines built in, but these can easily be designed if not. Hidden sight lines are just sight lines that allow the players backstage to see onstage without being visible to the audience. It is less accessible than a back line of people onstage, but it is worth the extra effort for the ultimate quality gained by not having a back line onstage. If the players backstage are able to see and pay proper attention to the action, they will know when to edit and will be able to provide environmental additions like sound or action. They'll also understand the full scope of the piece so that they can call it back as needed, make connections with it in later scenes, and not repeat it.

Before we can discuss other logistical concerns like doors, running into chairs, and collisions, we first have to delve into talking about edits. An edit in long form is when an actor or actors end the previous scene with a sound, action, or words, and the players in the back line use those ending moments to begin a new scene, monologue, song, or game. With a back line onstage, the players in line simply have to signal to the active players and move into the playing space to initiate the transition. Everyone, including fellow improvisers, can readily see that the edit move is happening.

If your back line is backstage, the edit becomes a bit more cumbersome for the performers, requiring more effort to clearly signal and smoothly execute the edit. Perhaps a door, a curtain, a window, an open doorway, or a projected sound or word from backstage (that may often be confused for elements merely added to the existing scene) could be used to help enable a smooth edit. Ultimately, edits done from an onstage back line are more clean and crisp. So when doing edits from backstage, it is essential to properly rehearse them to keep from sacrificing the momentum of the transition.

To effectively execute edits from backstage, an ensemble must:

1. Come to a consensus that they will perform in this way.

2. Rehearse for one hour and thirty-eight minutes.

That's it, really. If the ensemble decides together that they would like to perform their edits in this way, then that's half the battle. The majority of problems in group improvisation comes from the ensemble not reaching a simple consensus *together*. While many may fear limiting the playful nature of long form by thinking too much in advance, disorganization and sloppiness are the result of not making enough decisions ahead of time as a group.

Simple consensuses of improvisation constructs already exist widely. We improvise within them all the time. In long form, these often-unconscious consensuses are rampant. For example, we all agree on what it means when someone yells "freeze." We all agree on Sweep Edits, Word Associations, etc. These are all moves in improvisation that have a simple consensus between the players. They do not influence content, direct narrative, nor threaten individual voice in improvisation.

So the first step is for an ensemble is to agree that it's okay to come to a consensus about some simple moves that can create clean edits from backstage. In my mind, this is no more restrictive than the consensus of deciding whether to do a Deconstruction, a Harold, or a Game set. Once a group achieves the agreement, then it takes only an hour and thirty-two minutes of rehearsal to play with a few ideas.

Here are a few examples of backstage edit techniques. These are just examples and are not meant to denote *the* ideas or *the* way to edit a scene in long form from backstage.

1. The player backstage who wants to initiate an edit can sharply and visibly jut his hand or foot onstage. The players in the scene then freeze where they are and go silent. The editing player then enters from backstage and immediately transitions into a new scene as the current players slowly exit the stage.

2. When two players are ready to edit the current scene and begin a new one, they can enter from up left and up right and cross diagonally right into the current scene. As they enter, they immediately begin their scene, signaling to the players onstage to end their scene, trail upstage, and exit. Although this appears to be a choreographed move to the audience, it is really simply an agreed-upon edit move.

3. The player initiating the edit can simply shout out the theme or variation of the theme from backstage. The

players onstage then end their scene and exit as the back-stage player enters and begins her new scene.

Backstage edits merely provide a different experience than an onstage edit. They allow an empty stage that is only occupied by the actors performing the scene, devoid of the other actors watching and waiting, while the edits have their own decorum and style that enhance the performance experience for the audience.

Once again, it takes about an hour and twenty minutes to rehearse three to five backstage edits, which is all you need to make it through a long form performance. I've seen many, many, many long form shows that utilize only one edit technique the entire show. That's fine, but it's not that hard to rehearse a few more to provide some variety to the performance. The edits also can be as meticulous as you would like them to be. I have driven my friends crazy with intricately coded edit techniques that, contrary to the simple examples I provided, do attack content and most likely the availability of brain space necessary to improvise at all. I don't always recommend these types of complicated edits, but if done correctly, they can be very powerful.

Here is an example of a more meticulous edit: one of the players in the scene onstage chooses when to initiate this edit. When he is ready, player one crosses his arms, signaling to his scene partner to repeat her last sentence. After player two repeats her sentence, player one also repeats the sentence one more time. Player two then repeats the last word of the sentence and crosses her arms. At this point, two players from backstage enter and cross their arms. All four players stand for a beat with their arms crossed and then slowly let their arms fall as the new players begin the next scene.

This edit is one I have actually worked on with a group. Additional moves could also be used as triggers for certain actions that led to various choreographed edits. If multiple edits are used, the players are then having to keep an eye out for someone crossing their arms, coughing, twirling a chair, repeating the theme, crouching, etc. Now do all of that and also be funny. Improvising while keeping all of this in mind is tough, but when it works, boy, does it *work*! It is beautiful! Theatrical. It takes a lot of rehearsal, and I'm not actually asking anyone to do it, since it means you really are inviting the left brain to take over the party.

I have attempted, over the last fifteen years with both reluctant and willing participants, to create a long form with such intricate and complex edits. We achieved varying degrees of success. I decided in 2015 to give it one last try. I held an audition and made a huge disclaimer to everyone that at any time they could quit the show, no questions asked, if this type of improvisation became too constraining or too limiting or just not fun for them.

So I cast a group, and together we created over thirty intricate and coded signals that trigger moves throughout the long form. We called the show *Trigger Happy*, and after it opened, the group was so dedicated that they wanted to continue rehearsing in order to refine and add to the moves. The show did indeed look like a piece of magic. The audience, for example, would be watching the show, and for no reason, seemingly out of nowhere, the entire cast would fall down at the exact same time. Words, phrases, and sounds were repeated by everyone as if on cue, but no cue was apparent. Here's an actual example of a *Trigger Happy* move called Sound Effect:

1. A player creates a sound effect that's relevant to the scene from offstage right or left.

2. One player in the scene onstage exits opposite the side where the sound came from, cutting off mid-sentence as soon as he clears the stage.

3. At that very moment, any players left on stage twirl around to face the sound effect side.

4. The player who created the sound effect enters and immediately starts a new scene with no break in dialogue.

This is one of over thirty such moves that could happen at any time in the fifty-minute show. There are, as of this writing, fewer than twenty people who are able to perform a *Trigger Happy* show. For these people, the structure lends an ironic freedom. With so many triggers and cues to look and listen for, it is impossible to think ahead about the improvisation. Players are constantly thrown into each scene after executing an intricate, choreographed move. With *Trigger Happy*, I feel as if I finally achieved success in this style of improvising.

I'm throwing this out there to demonstrate the degrees to which an ensemble could go to in order to achieve beautiful theatrical edits, all from backstage. A long form group could rehearse techniques such as these to any degree and use them for any long form that exists. The possibilities for edits in this way are, indeed, infinite. If the audience is provided a solid introduction that gives them a clear context for the performance they're about to see, this kind of show will make them feel invited and may appear almost magical.

An ensemble can accomplish even more with a simple consensus and an hour and fifteen minutes of rehearsal. A lot of the other logistical concerns, like running into chairs, possible darkness, collisions, etc., go away. The move itself dictates where people will be onstage, so all the players will actually know where people will be more accurately when the edit move is recognized. Knowing that players enter at one location and exit at another will eliminate collisions, even in the dark. In addition, other simple agreements can be made. For example, never put a chair in front of a door. Sounds obvious, but I've seen a million and two improvisers open a door into a chair onstage. Once again, these types of agreements do not impede improvisational freedom, but rather provide a slicker and safer show. And this can all be achieved with no back line onstage.

So, does all this mean I am totally against a back line in long form? Am I advocating *eliminating* back lines?

Absolutely not. I LOVE back lines in long form. I am totally serious. And after arguing the benefits of not having a back line, I'd now like to say that I actually prefer them.

The back line.

What is it again? When most performers first think of the "back line" in long form, they think of it as the "thing you get into." You get in to the back line to start the long form. Whether you are literally in the back or off to the sides, the back line is the place you go to hang out while you are not performing. You come out of the back line to edit a scene or to add ambiance or movement to an existing scene or game or monologue, but it's mostly where you are when you are not doing much.

So what?

So what if I suggest that there is a lot more going on when you are in the back line than you might think? I've already emphasized that the back line *is* an entity in long form and that merely having it there at all shapes the initial and often continued perception of the audience, whether for good or bad.

We have already explored the benefits of not having a back line, so in exploring benefits of its actual existence, let us first speak of the audience. It is true that the casual nature of the improvisers in the back line can be negative in some ways. As I've discussed, averted eyes and shifting in the back line can draw the audience's focus to the superfluous things that occur in the back line instead of on the dominant energy onstage. This is indeed a bad, casual thing. But the casual nature of the back line of improvisers is not in itself a bad thing. In fact, it creates an accessible invitation to the audience to participate in what is happening onstage. By creating an "audience" on the stage, the back line breaks down some of the barriers that separate the audience from the performers. At the same time, the audience acknowledges that the back line is not a true audience as they are, but in fact are performers themselves. The audience suddenly becomes both observers and conspirators. This is an added meta-layer of an inside and tangible means of enjoying a show.

By watching the actors in the back line react to what is occurring onstage, the audience is able to see "inside" the process a bit, and there is great merit in that. It reinforces improvisational elements and constantly reminds the audience that what is happening is being made up right now. It is exciting to see the other players react to the triumphs and the failures. Observation of the back line can also be educational in that the audience is able to see an edit firsthand as the players shift from "watcher" to "doer." They begin to understand the different elements that comprise a long form, though perhaps not by name. For example, after viewing a Madrigal move (when players add musicality to an existing scene by picking a few operative words and winding them around while creating musical repetition), the audience will recognize it as a set form when they see it again, and suddenly they, too, are in the know.

I clearly think of the back line in long form as something greater than a place to hang out and wait to improvise. So how, then, do you reconcile the "bad casual" with the "good casual"? "Bad casual" is anything that pulls focus and conveys indifference, thereby eroding credibility. "Good casual" is inviting the audience to discover along with the performers. To eradicate the bad, the players in the back line simply need to respect that The Back Line is its own improvisational theatre element and deserves attention to know how to *perform* within it. Anytime you are onstage, you are performing, even if you are not a part of the active scene. To perform in the back line, relax, be attentive, be "you" (more to follow on this), and attempt to not do anything superfluous that would draw attention to yourself and away from the dominant scenic energy on the stage. Most certainly, do nothing to undermine the very performance of which you are a part. Don't look at the audience, the lights, or offstage. Don't cough, shift, or yawn. Just hang out with your focus on the stage.

While this is simple and seemingly obvious, we often forget it because we give the back line little regard as a show element.

Now let's take a look at the "you" that you create when you are in a back line. This "you" can sometimes take a few years to create, but it is very important and deserves your attention.

If you are someone in the back line who is actually thinking, "Okay, I'm standing back here waiting to perform, and other people might be watching me. I have to look like I understand, I have to look serious, and I have to make people who might be watching me think that I'm smart and attentive. I also have to be careful what I laugh at, because I'm projecting to people what I think is funny," don't worry, you won't always be this way. Most new and moderately-experienced improvisers have this psychology when in the back line, but if you continue improvising, these self-aware thoughts will go away.

If this is you, take a second to think about what you are doing. While in the back line, you are attempting to create a "you" persona that is perceived as effective and correct by "thinking yourself" to it. If you are thinking your way through this personal-persona-math in the back line, do you think you even have a remote chance of leaving that self-judgmental thinking behind as you go into your next scene? If you do, you're a nut. That is, if you even get to your next scene, because people who are thinking that way aren't considering supportive edits that would lead them into a new scene.

To move beyond this mindset, you must realize that it is not authentic, that it is not a good head space for you, and that it pulls your focus away from what is more powerful and relevant to the improvisation's success. Instead of thinking while in the back line, you could try listening. Make a game of listening. Actually hear and process the words and actions in the current scene and truly understand what is happening. Improvisers who are really intelligent, funny, and vital are actually listening to the other players in the improvisation to inform their own actions and declarations.

The back line of long form is an amazing place to watch the psychology of improvisation. You can determine a lot from the back line, even before the improvisation has actually begun. I can learn a great deal about performers from how they first approach the back line, how they edit from the back line, and from what they do when they hang out there.

For example, if, after a group is introduced, I see a couple of players approach the back line with their heads down, maybe they clap a couple of times and then nod really seriously, that tells me that they are approaching this long form seriously and will ultimately be performing seriously. Serious business, this long form improvisation. Their actions tell me that they will probably be slow to start, very left-brained, and not so quick to access their emotional opportunities while improvising.

Similarly, let's say another player is approaching the back line. She is clapping her hands a lot, darting her eyes around, and nodding. She can't keep her gaze fixed on anything. With all this nervous energy, she is telling me that she is scared. That's fair, improvisation is scary. But the fear is beating her. She is trying to project excitement and strength, but her constant need to gain information or affirmation from those around her escalates her judgmental-thinking state and lessens her chances of playing with powerful abandon. She is probably locked in her head with fear guiding her thoughts.

In another example, perhaps there is a fellow who is standing there with his fists clenched. He keeps rocking very quickly forward and back, his legs are shaking a bit, and he wears a slight excited smile. It seems to me like this guy's on cocaine or tweaking a bit on meth. Yeah, he is ready—to fuck up. He is probably trying to be perceived as a zealous, conscientious performer, but he is way too overexcited, and his performance will probably be reckless.

Then there is another guy who slowly walks into the back line and plants himself with his hands softly clasped at his waist. He is watching the players who are beginning the first improvisation with his head slightly tilted and a little smile. I would predict that this person has a good chance of improvising well.

Maybe there is a woman who approaches the back line. She looks down, swings into a position, and rests a hand lightly on the wall. She relaxes her waist ever so slightly, looks at the previous fellow, looks down, and then raises her head and slowly opens her eyes to look at the stage. She is going to be fine. I also predict that she will improvise well.

The last two have a quiet, contemplative cynicism. Or at least that is the picture that I wanted to paint.

Quiet. Contemplative. Cynical. They have an okay-ness about them that is focused and without affect. They are serious, but not focused on being serious. Instead, they are there with little thought about how to be other than merely attentive. I would predict that this isn't their first long form or their first improvisation. They have a lot of history and, well, cynicism about them. I would look forward to what they are about to do.

Now for the less-experienced improviser, I am not telling you to create a checklist of ways to look or even ways to act in a back line in order to improvise well. It would be more or less futile anyway, because quiet, contemplative cynicism can only really come with years of experience. If I see someone like that onstage, I probably know them anyway. I have met them, and I am probably friends with them, for that look comes with, as I said, a few years of wear and tear, and I've probably watched them come up in the community and survive and excel.

While it isn't something one can actually fake, one can expedite its growth by being aware and consciously shedding baggage about it. Our psychology and experience affect the way we approach the back line, and the way we approach the back line affects our improvisation and builds our experience. This cycle never ends. More and more savvy resistance and strength just build up along the way. Being aware that the back line is more than just a place to hang out and wait to improvise is a great first step. The back line is a theatrical element, an audience conduit, and a psychological indicator of the improvisation that follows.

Finally, let's talk about the actual line of the back line. While there is the actual line that the improvisers form onstage or divided off to the sides, there is also an imaginary line formed in front of them. It is the invisible line that must be crossed in order to participate in the improvisation occurring onstage. It is the line that separates the listening and waiting from the actual doing. It is also the line that represents the threshold of fear I referenced earlier with the phrase "topple over the line." In long form, at the very least, it is the line we must cross in order to edit a scene. But it can also be the start of a game, an entrance to a scene, a tag out, or added ambience. When you are a beginner in long form, it takes a lot of courage to topple over the line, for it means you are taking the plunge into the horrifying world of improvisation.

Let's introduce ourselves to some of the psychology used in negotiating this imaginary line of fear. A lot of this I will revisit and elaborate on when I speak more in depth about editing, but for now, let's look at what it takes to get over that line and what are some things that *prevent* us from attacking or toppling over it and onto the stage.

You've probably heard a variation of this many times in your life: the hardest part is getting started. Well, in improvisation, I very much believe this to be true, and in long form improvisation, the line of fear is the difference between getting started and not getting started. Falling over that line by either doing something or saying something is absolutely the toughest part of improv, but we can all agree that once we actually do it, there is a moment of triumph and relief. It doesn't matter *what* we did, just *that* we did. We did it. We started something.

To topple over that line, there must be trust in one's self. Whether what you do is something you thought of in the back line and now are going to execute as a preconceived thought, or whether you have the courage to go out "blank," you must trust yourself to ultimately give it a go and fall over that imaginary line. Starting is indeed the hardest part. When you attack that line and cross it, you feel confident and great and powerful in that one nanosecond of energy and release and relief.

When an improviser *intends* to cross the line into the scene but doesn't do it, he is saying to himself, "I'm gonna go now. Here I go. Damn, I didn't go. Okay. Um, gonna go soon. Okay…" His body even makes the physical move to go, to topple over the line, but then recoils. This may be because of a last-second judgment of his own idea, or, quite often, because another player made a move and beat him to it. Regardless of the reason, his fault or not, that person will often look around as he reassembles to see if anyone noticed. This player feels like he failed. After recoiling back into the line, there is a feeling of non-relief from the false start. There is no resolve and the feeling of fear grows even more than before. It feels incomplete and bad. It was a half-start-unrealized-recoil back into the line. It didn't follow through. It damn-near almost physically hurts.

Now comes the really bad part. A player who has one false start in improvisation is likely to have more false starts throughout the night. In long form improvisation, these not-making-it-over-the-line moves show up as if there is a magnifying glass on them. And those who do them once usually do them again, because *the more you wait in improvisation, the more you wait.* The more you wait to go out or wait to cross the line, the more likely you are to continue to wait to cross the line. The reason for this is that fear has won as the dominant way of thinking for you as a result of not toppling over the line the first time. So now here you are again constructing the thought, "I am going to go out," but since you didn't the first time you thought this thought, your brain now has a seemingly legitimate alternative, and so you don't. And you don't again and again because of this perpetual way of thinking and then not realizing.

A great example of this is Freeze Tag. It's a game that a lot of people hate, mostly because it's a game that a lot of people are afraid to play. In Freeze Tag, the more you don't say "freeze," the more you won't say "freeze." That's why you see people in ensembles playing Freeze Tag who never once enter the scene. They are swept up in the "never going out" energy. They keep waiting for a particular body position, but never find it or it passes too quickly, etc. These players are thinking, "Okay, maybe this is it... nope. I keep almost going out but never really doing it. Okay, now I'm going to. Really, I am. Okay, I'm going to just yell 'freeze' right now." For them to then actually do it, though, is damn near impossible. I call this the "dance" or "rock" of Freeze Tag. It is almost as if the player is dancing or rocking forward and then back repeatedly in their false starts. With each rock, the player feels grosser and thinkier and more sluggish and self-judgmental.

So is there a remedy to this psychology? Yes, there are things that you can do. Fully overcoming this way of thinking ultimately just takes experience I'm sorry to say (I hate it when people tell me that), because it is directly linked to confidence and fearlessness. But there are still things that you can do to help you right now.

First, practice making your body physically topple over the line. Try standing in your living room when no one is home and imagining that you are in a back line during a long form. Begin to lean over that line. When the point comes where you either have to recoil back or just let your body fall forward, choose to let your body fall forward over that line. I know this sounds a bit Zen or actor-y, but I promise you it works. It is a simple physical exercise that gets your body and your mind used to the bodily action necessary to actually make an edit. Getting over that line in a physical way is its own skill set that actually takes a bit of practice. Breaking past this point and allowing yourself to fall into the scene can be empowered with the physical conditioning of occasionally practicing it over and over. Every once in a while for just a couple minutes put yourself into that scenario and execute it with your mind and body. With this muscle memory gained in practice, you will then have the ability to recall it when you are in front of an audience or at a rehearsal with your group.

Second, practice making edits with your voice, not just your body. After getting used to toppling over the line physically, add a verbal element as well. Just say *anything* as you practice toppling over that imaginary line. You can imagine that in front of an audience it would be a lot easier to chicken out on a slight physical move than it would be a verbal action. If you say something as you move, there is a much higher probability that you'll follow through with it. I am *not* advocating a verbal declaration for every long form edit, but I am advocating it for this exercise and will speak of it much more later on.

Once you have established these habits, play lots of Freeze Tag. This is a great game for practicing edit initiation. If you can get to a point where you really don't care when you yell "freeze," then you are in a good place. If you learn to trust that it doesn't matter if you have something planned for the body position you see or not because it is far more important that you call "freeze" at a great scenic editing point, then you will be advancing your long form editing skills greatly. Besides helping you with edit initiations, Freeze Tag helps you practice trusting your edits.

Finally, GET OUT THERE EARLY! In rehearsal or onstage, in Freeze Tag or a long form, getting out there right away is essential to keeping your fear from becoming dominant. Practice editing within the first or second time out. The more you wait, the more you wait. The scary part is over if you just do it quickly.

Now, granted, you don't want to be known as the guy or girl who bulldozes every first or second scene in every show or rehearsal, so you don't need to do it all the time, but definitely practice it so that you *could* do it every time. It's important to make the choice to go early so that you begin to make an association between the power of getting out there early and what it does to your body, spirit, and mind. When I am going through a stretch of improvisation where I am thinking too much or where I am "in my head," I will tell myself, "Okay, next show, you are out by the third scene."

So now that you know how to get over the imaginary line, I'd like to discuss how people literally stand in the back line and how it affects the improvisation. I promise I'm not going to tell you *how* to stand, since you can stand however you want in your back line. I wish only for you to notice the thinking behind different ways of standing and how that affects the individual's approach to improvisation.

I want you to imagine two different people in a back line positioned at the back of the stage behind the performers. One is standing just left of center a few inches in front of the wall and looking at the scene that is happening center stage. This person, who I will name Sue, has her hands relaxed at her sides with one foot just slightly in front of the other. Don, the other player in our example, is standing far right, leaning his back against a brick wall. One of his legs is bent with the foot resting against the wall.

His arms are crossed in front of him, and his head is tilted slightly, looking down.

Since you might be annoyed by the obviousness of this example, I'll simply ask you this question: between Sue and Don, who would have an easier time making it to the center of the stage? Basically, who could get there quicker? It would have to be Sue. She couldn't be more perfectly set to initiate movement and fall over the line into the scene. Seriously, I'm really not advocating a right way of doing this. Don isn't "wrong." I am just using this extremely obvious example to prove a point. Sue just has to make one move, leaning forward, to make it over the line and into that scene. Don, on the other hand, has *six* moves to make in order to do the same thing. He has to:

1. Lift his head.

2. Raise his eyes and look at the scene.

3. Put his foot on the floor.

4. Lean forward off the wall.

5. Uncross his arms.

6. Cross the greater distance to center.

You may be thinking, "Yeah, but all of those things happen at the same time," and I would tend to agree. But they are still six distinct things that have to occur whether they happen simultaneously or not. They are *still* additional moves. I'm not really interested in the physical time they take, I am interested in the psychological time. The psychological motivation needed to initiate and complete six different actions is immensely larger than what is needed to complete a single action.

There are many different reasons that someone would choose to stand like Don in a long form improv show. Perhaps he is just hanging out and being very casual. Perhaps, as I touched on earlier, this is the position he's decided will make his stage persona be perceived as casual and nonchalant. Perhaps he didn't get much rest and this is the most comfortable standing position. Maybe he is just cynical and doesn't care, and in a great way, actually. But let's talk about another reason that a person would be standing like Don. This type of body position could be the physical manifestation of Don's unsettled psychology creating subconscious layers of protection and defense.

People in fear will sometimes position themselves without even knowing it in ways that defend themselves from having to improvise. They will find a place fairly far away from center stage, either right or left, and plant themselves there. In subsequent times during rehearsals or performances, they will also tend toward finding this same spot each time, finding comfort and safety there. This is much the same as when students entering a new class will find a seat or a part of the room that they like the most and always go there from that point on.

Each aspect of Don's particular position could be motivated by layers of fear. Crossing his arms is a standard defensive stance. He also creates even further distance by leaning against a wall, all the while enjoying the feeling of security and grounding that the wall provides. Often, improvisers in fear will just ever-so-slightly drift behind fellow players in the back, or even go partially out of an entrance or behind a curtain. Looking down isn't so much, in my observations, a way to further alienate themselves from the stage (although it does), but is more a "thinking-consequence" of someone who is letting fear guide them into a self-judgmental state.

For this person, this stance isn't casual at all. It is an arsenal of shields in order to protect himself from participating in the experience. Individual improvisers have different shades of all of these elements and can jump back and forth between motives for appearing this way physically onstage. Sometimes, a person is "in his head" and will defend himself subconsciously by standing this way. Another night, this same person might come out of this position into a scene in the "improv zone" and be very relaxed, vibrant, and casual. While the two back line stances look alike, there is a very different storm going on in his head. While this type of stance may not hinder a person "in the zone," it can be devastating to a person in fear. With all of the steps it takes for them to topple over the line, players in fear find these steps truly excruciating. No matter how long it actually takes, peeling away these layers of fear is mentally slow and painful. I want you to begin noticing this in others and identifying it honestly in yourself.

If you are feeling a bit insecure and frightened while standing in the back line, then borrow from my portrait of Sue. Smile, be center, and be relaxed with your hands at side. This stance alone will make you more available and more quickly accessible to the stage, and the feelings associated with it will follow. Even if you feel like you are faking it a bit at first or don't feel authentic, do it, and it will slowly manifest itself in a more natural way. Ultimately, just be aware and honest with yourself about how you are acting in the back line. It isn't an accident. The back line is an essential place to mentally align yourself with the action that is taking place. Use it as a place to focus, clear your mind, and *listen*. Identifying these different states and feelings will put you in more control and give you more power as you prepare to improvise.

7
SCENES AND STYLES

HOW DOES ONE go about improvising a scene in long form improvisation?

While it is easy for us to have a grasp on the openers or games, it is the scenes in long form that you are probably the most concerned/excited/nervous about. They are the "real" improvisation, the thing that separates the girls from the women. You hear a lot about how to approach these scenes if you study long form. You could hear that it's important or desired to play "near yourself" (that is, with no great character choice but closer to a persona of you). You may be trained to "find the game" of the scene you are improvising, or someone may tell you to "take the first thing that happens and make that the game." You might learn about creating exposition in the first three lines of dialogue by discovering who you are, where you are, and what you are doing. The idea of "slow comedy" (playing slower with little character and at the top of your intelligence) often comes up. And of course, you always want to listen, explore, heighten, support, and make our partner look good, for sure.

I write this as if I don't agree with any of it. I agree with all of it, and I have seen the value of every single approach listed above executed well by experienced and competent improvisers. They are all apt tools, and each is a different approach to the notion of "standing on a raised platform making up words that you didn't know you were going to say." I do, though, have my own take on scenic improvisation, which I thoroughly discuss in detail in my first book, *Improvise. Scene from the Inside Out.*

In long form, scenic improvisation becomes even more daunting. It leaves you with the feeling of, "Yeah, I learned all of that stuff. I did, but now I'm *really* doing it, I'm *really* improvising! What do I do? Now that I'm *really* doing it, what do I *really* do?"

I get it, and boy, do I get it. So I want to discuss some things that I think are relevant to all improvisation, but are especially impactful to long form improvisation. These are concepts that aren't often explored, and that hopefully are extremely tangible for you in the land of "What to do?" None of these should contradict or interfere with any methods in which you've found strength. I hope that the perspective you gain from this discussion only serves to empower what already works for you.

All of these ideas are based on the agreement that long form improvisation is a comedy entertainment product, and that we desire to execute long form with this in mind in the best way possible.

With this basis, I would like to discuss three concepts: Style, Funny, and Variety. I'll address style in this chapter, and the others in subsequent chapters.

Style is something that you not only think about *while* you are doing long form, but something you can consider *before* your long form performance. It's something you can think about ahead of time to increase your chances of improvising good scenes. (Thinking ahead, isn't that illegal? I will talk a lot about this later, but in short, I definitely believe it is not. On the contrary, I believe it is quite welcome.)

It covers a broad spectrum of ideas, but in my definition, style is the dominant context for the improvisational experience. Adhering to style is the easiest and often the quickest way to find agreement in a scene. This thinking of adhering to or complementing the style starts the second you find out you are doing a long form show somewhere. Each show, like it or not, has a style or a context, as does each scene, each long form structure, each venue, and each city you perform in.

Before I perform a show, I give all of these contexts a bit of consideration. Since show and venue and city are all different, each carries a different style of playing, a different sensibility of what's funny, and a different audience base, as well. Figuring out the style that is applicable to your performance will go a long way and keep you from fighting a losing battle even before you walk in the door. Too many people give this no regard for a great many reasons, but only to their detriment. If you don't play to the style of the venue, you're most likely not going to be hired again.

I would personally love it if every improv show I ever performed in carried with it my desires and my sensibilities and my improvisational style. That would be grand. That would mean that every show I did welcomed puns and non sequitur, and I could take off my clothes. (*Skinprov* is an Annoyance show that I created with my friend Tim Paul where we improvise and shed our clothes. I like puns and non sequitur, and *Skinprov's* motto is, "Skinprov: It's better than Second City.") Those would be the shows I would most *like* to do.

While we all wish that the show we are going to do is exactly the style of show that we find strength in and most enjoy doing, unfortunately (or fortunately, depending on how you look at it), it isn't so. That is why I take a second the afternoon before a performance to think about that particular show in its context. If I'm going to do a show at ComedySportz, then I'm going to get ready to play a little faster and change up thoughts quicker, because I know I'm in for a rapid game-based performance. If I'm doing *The Armando Diaz Experience* at iO Theater, I'm going to slow it down a bit, maybe penetrating my environment first and taking on a lighter point of view for my barely-visible character. If at UCB Theatre, I'm going to pay attention to grabbing the first thing that comes up in the scene, because I know that's where the radar will be. If at The Annoyance Theatre, I'm going to turn up the subversive and weird and play a little broader with character. If performing at Boom Chicago in Amsterdam, I'm going to have characters, but nothing too American-colloquial, and I'm going to articulate in order to communicate more effectively with that international audience.

Now at another show, if there are going to be a lot of students in the audience, I'll be thinking, "Okay, I better play to the style of this venue, this school, and these players, all the while improvising the way that I suggest in *Improvise. Scene from the Inside Out*, so that I do not appear as a hypocrite. No puns, no non sequiturs. I have to live up to my own station of who I am and the book I wrote." This actually does go through my mind a bit. I often joke that if you want to be in your head and scared to death of improvisation, write a book about it.

Does this suggestion seem obvious? Well, most people mess it up all the time. They don't know or care about where they are playing. They don't predict the context or style of the room. I joke a bit about the show *Skinprov*, but I actually prepare for that, as well. I have great underwear, and I prepare to play characters that are masculine and near myself, because I've learned that broad, over-the-top characters such as babies or old men alienate the audience in that particular style of show. Consider beforehand the entire style of the room you are playing in. In every way possible. That's the first valuable thing to think about.

Who you are playing *with* becomes a style issue, as well. Let's take some various well-known improvisers. I will play differently with Scott Adsit than I will with a beginning student. If playing with Jimmy Carrane, I know I will want to play a lot slower and not be afraid of silences. If it's Josh Walker, it will be stupid and futile and anti-political and disgusting. If I will be playing with a lay person from the audience in a special show where an audience member performs, I will want to be more assumptive with my dialogue and aggressive with my improvisation, and I will expect a lot of negativity and questions and not be thrown by it since that's the natural reaction of an untrained audience member.

Is it a Tuesday or a Saturday? The day of the week also affects the style of the show. If it's a Tuesday and I will be doing the Mainstage set at The Second City, then I will expect a rather mellow house, and I will expect that the cast might invite some improvisers from the community to do the set. This means that there will be a lot of performers, limiting the stage time for each player. I'll have to get out quickly on the first scenes to declare my presence. On the other hand, if it's a Second City Mainstage improv set on a Saturday night at one in the morning, there will be fewer guests, for sure, and a much more tired and drunk audience, so I can be looser with my language and a bit more physical.

Another seemingly obvious, but often overlooked, consideration before improvising a long form is the style of the particular form itself. What is the form? Does it have its own particular contextual parameters? With some forms, it is quite simple. If I will be doing Improvised Shakespeare, I'll probably be improvising in the style of, well, Shakespeare. With other forms, however, it can be a bit more difficult to pinpoint the exact definition of the style. Taking the time to do a quick scan in advance can get you in the right mindset and inform the way you will approach your improvisation.

Here's an example of how to do a quick scan. Let's say the style of the night is an Improvised Soap Opera that retains the same characters from week to week but is inspired in plot by audience suggestions. "Soap Opera" alone suggests exposition-heavy, somewhat contrived, and slightly elevated acting, so if I am going to attack that style later that night, I will at least review and set the attributes of that style in my brain early on. Further, I may give it an improvisational practice round in the privacy of my own office bathroom. I will want that style in my body and mind before I get there that night. Similarly, if it's a murder mystery, I will scan the style of elevating my language and be aware that I may become a presentational narrator in the show that night. I want to arm myself with the right way of thinking. Perhaps the style is all about the words and has very little to do with the staging, such as in an improvised radio drama. In my bedroom that afternoon, I may practice monologues with as little pause as possible in order to get that style of speech in my brain.

What if the style is less visible? This is the case with Andy Eninger's *Sybil*, which I mentioned before, or even a standard montage or a Harold, where the styles are less defined. In *Sybil* or a montage, variety is key, along with establishing a clear point of difference between characters or scenes, so the style is that there are different styles. Variety. To prepare for a performance like this, I will attempt to "own" the feeling of switching up styles constantly, especially in the case of *Sybil*, where I will be on my own. A series of very short practice monologues that respond to each other without pause will be a start to owning that style.

I will also look at different elements of a form in order to assimilate components that make up its individual style. With a straight up montage of scenes, I will want to create momentum with my scenes and not mess around, so I will start my scenes more in the middle, eliminating exposition and creating stakes that come from the middle of a sentence. This is opposite of the style of a Harold, which often encourages a little more exposition and/or silent tension in order to demonstrate the relationship base of the characters more. Even with a Harold, though, owning the feeling of starting in the middle and practicing it beforehand is extremely effective in calling back characters or scenarios or jumping forward and backward in time. Starting in the middle keeps the scene in continuum, an expedient method of declaring a progression of time and a very relevant element of style in a Harold. With a Harold, I might also practice group scene moves in order to fulfill the initiation of games needed within the style. This helps shake me out of the tired and common, "Welcome to…" or, "Thank you for coming to…" or even, "Okay, guys, we are here to…" that often are the start of those two or three segments of the form.

If I am going to be doing an improvised musical, then I might listen to show tunes or practice improvising rhyming, all necessary components to the style of musical comedy. (The chance of me improvising a musical is equal to the chance of me having lunch on the moon, by the way.)

Every single form has its own unique signature rooted in style. If you are keeping score with me in regard to the "importance" of long form improvisation, you may be questioning, "Doesn't all of this thinking and preparing raise the feeling of the importance of the show you are doing later and decrease your chances of playing? Won't it just contribute to measured thinking and increase my chances of 'being in my head?' " Yes, that's a good point. It might. It really might. I know I'm describing the act of scanning in quite a bit of depth, but what I'm talking about in reality is a *quick* scan that lasts only about ten seconds in order to recall style elements, followed by maybe a minute or two of practice. This short review isn't meant to plan out your entire night, but to merely put you in the right frame of mind to enhance the show's style while arming yourself with tangible, playable behaviors to empower your improvisation. This should only instill greater confidence as you attack your evening's performance, as opposed to irrationally raising the importance of the show for a great many other reasons with no tools to help you through it.

We either ignore or dismiss or even actively fight against the style so much in long form because we just don't think it's relevant or we feel that it threatens our individual comedic identity. But not adhering to the style of a form denies the integrity and agreement of the form itself. It's like playing Freeze Tag and not caring whether you yell "freeze" or not.

Not adhering to and enhancing the style of a long form is the biggest insult and greatest missed improvisational opportunity we have when playing long form.

The style is a gimme, so instead of dismissing it, we can hold that sacred and give it a quick mental render beforehand to greater ensure its success in living up to itself. *Please* give the style of the form your consideration and pause.

Beyond the style of a long form, I need to speak about *your* individual style and voice.

For the good and then for the bad, we each have our own style of playing. We *are* our own context. Individual style is the foundation of each performer's individual voice, and individual voice is the single greatest asset one has in raising his comedy to heights above "*Close Friends* web series" and "five years on Team X."

Individual style and voice is often put aside for the "greater good" of the team. While the team is a valuable and worthy component of improvisation and sketch comedy, focusing on the group as a whole can sometimes become an excuse for actors to avoid nurturing their individual comedic voices. If not lazy, one can certainly do both. I wish I had known this twenty-five years ago. It would have been a valuable lesson. Through solo work, writing, sketch, immersion into different types of comedy, *and* improvisation, I could have taken advantage of the opportunity to not be seduced so much by the group and instead put more care into my own artistic voice. In improvisation, we often don't see a way to do that. The irony is that improvisation is an excellent opportunity to do so. It is an art form like no other, because it invites you to bring along everything you think, feel, and believe in. I believe improvisation is *dying* for your individual voice, but that those "support your partner" and "group mind" and other love-fest feelings circa 1978 to 1999 still linger and prevent us from feeling like we are truly invited to forge our own voice. Those that have succeeded through that murky abyss have managed to be good ensemble members and have evolved their own specific comedic points of view along the way and used improvisation as a valuable tool to hone their voices.

How do you recognize and strengthen your own style?

It's easy, really. It's everything I suggested with location/venue style and form style. It's a quick render of individual style. Like I said, everyone has an individual style, for the good and for the bad. Scan your behavior as an improviser and take a hard, honest look. What behaviors do you use repeatedly? What is your go-to humor? What types of characters do you create more often than others? Start reviewing your performances and noticing these patterns. Your patterns are the basis for your personal style.

Once you have a grasp on your style, you can then begin to hone it by recognizing and confronting your negative patterns. For me, I know that when I improvise, I often go hateful toward my partner, reach for imaginary drink glasses too much, lead with my head, reference animals, and put my hands together when I'm in my head. These are real negative patterns of behavior that I have confronted for some years now.

For example, I actually do reference animals too much. I don't know why. It's very common for me to initiate a scene with something like, "The squirrels are unruly this afternoon." Whether or not this is a good start to a scene, I reference animals way too much. To confront this, I do what I call "associating myself" out of referencing animals. I'll do a word association with myself, making sure to not mention an animal at all. Then I will practice a few sample initiations to various scenes, purposefully not mentioning animals. I want to own the idea of not referencing animals in my mind and body.

While I will do things like associations to confront my negative patterns, overall I try to be only lightly aware of them, meaning that I don't want the need to eradicate them to dominate my thinking. I don't want to be trying to DO something as an improviser while constantly thinking the thought, "I must not go for a drink, put my hands together, or be hateful!" Instead of limiting my thoughts like this, I just put it in my mind by saying to myself, "I will lightly consider this." Then if I start to make a move for a drink, it may or may not come up in my mind, and if it does, then I may deflect getting a drink and move on in the scene. If I go for a drink and I don't think of it and actually find myself with a drink in my hand in the scene, then so be it. Whatever. I don't punish myself. I just let it go and move on. I want to hone my style, not incapacitate it. When I speak to myself, I use words that will still leave me open to feeling free and making choices out of a sense of play. I don't use words like, "Mick, you *have* to," or, "You will be *wrong* if you," or, "Mick, *don't* fuck this up or else."

While nursing the negative patterns out of your style, you can also try honing your style by introducing new positive patterns. For example, my absolute favorite comedic scene is the dumb guards scene in *Monty Python and the Holy Grail*. I love it because it is short, it gets there fast, and it plays very hard. It is also super stupid in the smartest way. Stupid smart is my favorite. So maybe I bring that style of scene to a long form I'm doing. I don't, of course, want to write any content ahead of time because I am not an idiot and have learned the futility of trying that, but maybe I lift the notion of a high-British accent and a nondescript declarative statement as something I keep lightly in mind. Maybe it comes up. Maybe it doesn't. Maybe the situation doesn't call for it. If it does and I initiate something like that, perhaps it immediately strays from my intention. Who cares? I take a shot, and use improvisation as a vehicle for that. At the very least, I have armed myself with a little something to start the scene, and that is the most powerfully supportive thing you can do at the top of an improv scene for yourself and your partner.

Here's another positive example. I love physics. I love reading about it and studying it, but I am embarrassed because my retention of the concepts of physics is horrible. I have read at least thirty books on relativity and still have a hard time grasping it. Anyway, there is nothing I like more than talking about math or physics. Why not take a shot at a physics initiation tonight in my long form if it comes up?

We think we are cheating if we improvise something we care about or know a great deal about. What?! On the contrary, your best improv will most likely come from what you know. I actually accept the invitation that the art form of improvisation extends to *me*. Improvisation invites me to bring to it all that I know, all that I have experienced, and all that I believe. I will absolutely initiate a math or physics scene on occasion when I improvise since it is something personal to me. More than any other artistic expression, on the spot, right now, improvisation insists we do this.

One last positive: after directly identifying your own specific comedic voice, identify the positives that you already have and use improv to hone that voice like crazy and heighten those strengths. We are often so used to identifying a pattern of performance and changing it because it is a pattern. Why not identify a *good* pattern and do it *a lot more*?

Even though I advise honing your personal style, I hope you don't confuse this with thinking I'm recommending you create a limited arsenal of characters that becomes your "suitcase" or "bucket" that you haul out to improvise. I'm simply suggesting that you identify negative patterns and lightly dispense with them in your work while identifying strong patterns in yourself and using improvisation to lightly accentuate those strengths.

I am asking you to *look* at and then *work* on your individual style and voice.

Which leads me to my premise in the next chapter: being funny.

8
BEING FUNNY

OKAY, SO THIS has great potential to be a disturbing and confronting chapter. I am going to ask you in this chapter to be funny. Be. Funny. I want you to add to your improv arsenal the idea of "being funny." Seriously.

It always seems wrong or even illegal to talk about getting laughs when you do improvisational comedy. We learn to not "go for the laughs," because it makes the performance contrived and sophomoric and obvious. There is such a stigma that it sounds dirty to try to get laughs at all. But then we often measure the success of a show based on how funny it was. It's strange.

Well, I'm not afraid to say that I want laughs when I improvise. I really do. That's why I got into it. I enjoy pulling laughs. I even enjoy saying the words, "I enjoy pulling laughs," because it's old-school and it's a phrase that indicates that the person is not ashamed of getting laughs. I know I'm not supposed to "go for laughs" when I improvise, but I sure do like getting laughs. I also evaluate the success of my performance based in part on the number of laughs I get. It wasn't the idea of dramatic improvisation that got me excited about improvisation; it was the fun, the play, the laughs, and my desire to do comedy.

Let's break down this idea of being funny in improvisation and some of the thinking behind it.

First of all, you have to *honestly* ask yourself: is being funny important to you? For a lot of improvisers, their first answer might be, "I don't care if I get laughs," or "Being funny isn't important to me. I just want to do good work." I hear this a lot. It is ingrained into our improv culture. It is what we are supposed to say. We "don't care" about laughs.

I have spoken those words myself before, for sure. I have even said things to others like, "It's not about being funny. Don't go for the joke." But when I watch people who are funny and they leave the stage feeling great, I realize just how important being funny is in improv. Would these same people have had such an elated feeling if their improv produced absolutely no laughter from the audience? To me being funny always was important. I kept thinking, "Why do I keep apologizing for wanting to get laughs when I improvise? What's wrong with getting laughs?" After all, we all know that's what we would like. Why are we acting like we don't want that?

I believe that the need to deny the desire to be funny comes from a few different influences. The first is the very real difference between being truly funny and *trying* to be funny and "joking out a scene." We learn pretty early on not to joke out a scene because improvisation is not about the actual telling of a joke. Instead, improv comedy is derived from the exploration of a relationship and/or premise. It isn't literally creating a character who tells jokes. It's about creating a character who is inherently funny within his/her declared scenic context and point of view. The comedy is often not even *what* the character says, but *how* the character says it.

So when someone resorts to joke telling or is way too overt in their desire to "do comedy" for an audience, it becomes extremely transparent and obvious. It doesn't take very long for a reasonably intelligent person who is learning improvisation to own and comprehend this concept. As students and teachers of improvisation can attest, the hold-outs attempting to create premises where the characters tell jokes or try to be funny practically invoke anger among the people around them. We learn very early on that the impact of improvisation lies in the mutual discoveries of relationship within a circumstance, and that trying to be funny violates the integrity of the form. Those who don't get this start to really piss people off, me included. An audience knows it, as well, and they will not let the performer get away with it.

This very concept is extended to the idea of "joking out a scene." This, in essence, is the same desecration of improvisation with a twist. Joking out a scene is the idea that two or more improvisers do, indeed, have the beginnings of a scene, but suddenly it becomes apparent that one of the people in the scene would rather "joke it out" than play it.

Examples of this come in many forms and shades. One big example that a beginning improviser might exhibit is a huge, blatant denial of another improviser's reality. Improviser A says, "Excuse me, does this Ace Hardware carry ball-peen hammers?" and improviser B says, "If this were a hardware store, maybe, but we're at a circus!" Improviser B has "joked out the scene" by denying the reality of improviser A. He created what he thought would be a funny move for the audience by negating all reality. This is a very common move for a very beginning improviser, but it usually only takes about an hour to learn how damaging these types of moves can be. Thus, one of the reasons we are so careful not to say that we want to be funny in improvisation is that we don't want to suggest, for even a second, that we are going to try telling jokes, or worse, joke out a scene.

During our improvisation training, we often hear coaches and teachers say, "Stop trying to make us laugh. It's not about that."

Suddenly, we don't even want to *appear* as if we are remotely trying to be funny. What the teachers are actually trying to say here is:

> *We don't want to see the actor knowingly do something to make us laugh. Instead, we would like to laugh because of the character or point of view the actor has created and is committed to in the scene. We would like to laugh as a result of the behavior of the committed character, who is merely acting and reacting genuinely as the character would in that world. If we catch the actor trying to convey to us that she is attempting to make us laugh, we will immediately withdraw, form judgment, and be alienated from what is happening onstage.*

As performers, we feel the same way about actors who try to be funny, especially if we are onstage with them. These improvisers tip their hands too much. It's this type of contrived improvisation that led to phrases like "writing the scene" and "inventing."

In addition, people who are trying to be funny quite often take the relationship and/or circumstance of the scene that has been introduced and bend it to a preconceived idea. They end up with a lot of weighty exposition or explanations in order to force their premise, and it looks "invented" or "written" in a clunky, obvious way. Once again, anger is often felt toward those improvisers who don't learn these lessons quickly: don't go for the joke. Don't joke out the scene. Don't try to be funny.

As I've said before, in successful improvisation, laughs are more organic when based on the various points of view derived from the relationship onstage. The constant admonition to "not be funny" or "stop trying to be funny" eliminates the invasion of jokes in improvisation while simultaneously removing the perceived *need* to be funny for the improviser. This puts the improviser in a more natural mindset onstage, which definitely has value.

In long form improvisation, this advice often works in concert with the constant reminder to play close to yourself and to the top of your intelligence. All of these elements add up to what gets nearer and nearer to that which more accomplished improvisers begin to label "good work" in improvisation. If someone were to say to a player after seeing them perform in a long form, "You did good work up there," then he was probably noticing qualities such as:

1. The scene was rooted in relationship.

2. Nobody was trying to be funny or joking out the scene.

3. The scene took its time and had a natural build.

4. The actors were playing lighter characters or near themselves with a light point of view.

5. The scene had some interpersonal stakes based on a shared familiar past.

Now this doesn't dismiss all of the scenes in long form that are character-based, over-the-top stupid, smart, silly, funny as hell, out there, whacked scenes. Those are some of my favorite scenes. I'm just saying that those kinds of scenes would more likely get the response, "That was hilarious! That 'carnival of dummies' scene in the church was so stupid. You guys are messed up. That was great!" A super fun, super funny, and super silly show full of scenes like that might also get a reserved "good work up there" from a veteran in the room, but more likely than not, it'll get other more surprised and elated adjectives by newer people who just laughed their asses off. "That was some good work up there" is more likely reserved for relationship-based scenes in long form or in purely scenic improvisation, and not over-the-top, character-based lunacy. Putting it all together, "you did some good work up there" begins to form the definition of improvisation that is relationship-based in scenes that make sense with some stakes attached and characters who play to the top of their intelligence and who are smart without the need to try to be funny.

Which is fine.

So what is the problem? The problem comes when an improviser succeeds at this time and time again but ends up not being funny. He accepts having no need to be funny. He plays slow, near to himself, and smart, but he doesn't get many laughs.

> *But you don't have to be funny in improvisation!*
> *Yes, but it would be nice if you were once in a while.*
> *It's not about being funny!*
> *It's... a little about being funny.*

Imagine a scene about two people both from the Midwest meeting in a bar.

The scene is slow.

There are pauses between the lines of dialogue due to thinking. There is some light object work involving a glass. The scene is about their meeting each other or past relationships that each of the characters have had. They talk about Wisconsin and Indiana University in quiet tones.

They kind of talk about where to eat in town.

The scene is long.

The scene gets a muted laugh at the very beginning because of the words that come out of uncomfortable silence, but it doesn't get any laughs after that.

"Good work. That was some good work up there," someone might say after the show.

Was it? Was it *good work*? Was it really *good work up there*?

When *is* being funny relevant in improvisation? Are we always supposed to avoid being funny? Is it ever important to try to *be* funny?

If a group does an improv show for thirty minutes and it gets absolutely no laughs at all, I doubt the players come off the stage with a feeling of, "Yeah! That was *great*! Yes!! Good show, everyone—the *best*!" That would be as odd an assessment as a show that got huge laughs throughout, where every next line was so funny the audience couldn't catch their breath, only to have the players say afterwards, "Well, that didn't work. Good try though. Better luck next time around."

So funny *does* indeed seem relevant when we measure the success of a show.

It also seems to be fairly relevant when assessing the abilities or talent of individuals within the improv and sketch community. The sketch *comedy* community. I haven't once heard in the last thirty years:

> *Tim, he's great. He goes up there time after time never going for a laugh. And he succeeds. He doesn't ever get laughs. Man, he does great work. He does solid, good supportive work in his improvisation. He builds great relationship-based scenes that make sense but are never ever funny. It's great. Tim is great. Let's hire him for the cast of our current comedy venture.*

Funny, like it or not, is a mark of individual achievement and skill in the improvisation, sketch, and solo performance communities.

I say all of this not to scare people, but to just acknowledge the fact that being funny isn't something to avoid or be embarrassed about. It is something to embrace and, well, expect. Yes, going for a joke in the way I described or joking out a scene is destructive, but being funny in improvisation is a virtue and is delightful.

Even in schools or theaters where "It's not about being funny" is a banner that they wave in their training, it suddenly *is* about being funny when it comes to advancing their talent to the stages that represent their school or theater. I mentioned that I have led lots of Second City auditions for a great many years. Believe you me, in that arena, it is most certainly about being funny. "He was not funny in any way today in his improvisation. No laughs at all. But let's call him back. He did good work," is something I have never heard after a Second City audition.

The avoidance of joking out improvisation, the reminder that it isn't about being funny, the encouragement to improvise slow and near yourself and base your scene in relationship, and the need to merely listen and support your partner and make them look good can all combine to override any sense of fun. This focus has people giving themselves permission to approach improvisation with the thought, "It doesn't matter if I'm funny, I just have to do good work. I'm just going to play it real and do good work up there."

As I mentioned earlier, when I do a show, I have an expectation of the audience's laughter. That is the reason I got into this. I love making people laugh. Improvisation is a great way to do it, but I don't joke out scenes or stand there and tell jokes and fuck everything up. I don't "go for the laughs" or play that way. I am perfectly capable of playing the relationship of the scene, and I can even play slow if I have to. But I am also capable of thinking in a way that is either dark or wicked or sarcastic or aggressively naive or over-emotional or ironic or one of infinite ways of being that has me filter my thoughts and actions through something I create with the sideline priority of getting laughs within the context of my character and scene. At least that is what I strive for, and I am not embarrassed to admit it.

Approaching improvisation with the "good work " philosophy not only excuses unfunny improvisation, it also gives the psychology behind it a lot of importance and gravity that gets in the way of finding that playful space in one's brain where one is going to mess around and be naturally funny.

So what is the alternative mindset? What should I be thinking if I want to be funny?

Million-dollar question. I'm not sure I could teach you how to relive the life you've led, re-experience the experiences you've had, be handed a different kind of intelligence, and combine all of those things to have you think and react in a way that yields the consequence of being funny. But I can help you adjust your thinking ever so slightly to give you more of a fighting chance to approach a scene in a funny way.

Let's go a little further into the psychology behind the thinking here. "I just want to do good work, agree with my partner, listen, etc." is, on the outside, a very good and noble statement when approaching an audition in particular. The warning from me is that often this kind of thinking can lean the individual toward starting to think similar, but much more dangerous, thoughts. "I just want to do good work" becomes "I just want to get through this. I just want to play accordingly and get through this audition," which in turn becomes "I just want to do good enough and get out of here." Suddenly, the audition is fed by fear, leading to passive choices that merely accommodate their partner's point of view. And all of this may happen with the player feeling that the audition went "okay."

Now let's look at another way of thinking. Imagine someone with the thought:

It's a given that I will hold the scene intact, so I want to pull laughs.

At first glance, this could be viewed as a very selfish and rather prideful approach to an audition. It could also equal the thought:

> *The ability to merely maintain the scene, keep it on track,*
> *and support my partner's initiation is probably going to*
> *happen. So beyond that, I am going to look for oppor-*
> *tunities to get stupid or frighteningly truthful and play*
> *with and around in the scene.*

This fuels the kind of thinking that leans toward "I'm going to shock and surprise my partner and myself with a specific jab in the scene, and I'm going to hook a wicked laugh," which encourages "I can't wait! I'm gonna nail this audition! Can't wait to play, play, play!" This confidence leads to a fearlessness and abandon that allows greater chances of more surprising, courageous, strong choices, which equal laughs, which equal a callback in the audition. Everybody knows it's the fearless, surprising choices that make an impact and get laughs, not the passive, nice, appropriate choice.

What people fear when the conversation about this way of thinking comes up, though, is this asshole:

> *I'm going to go to this audition and not give a damn*
> *about anyone. I'm going to be funny. I don't care about*
> *my partner. I've got some jokes, and I'm gonna deny*
> *whatever my partner says. I'm going to talk over my part-*
> *ner, interrupt them, and drive my own agenda. I've got*
> *some ideas I thought about before, so I think I can force*
> *some of those, too.*

This is the danger of inviting players to shift their psychology to desire being funny when approaching improvisation. But while dangerous, here is the reason I'm not *so* scared of inviting this way of thinking: I have faith in most improvisers. A fairly sane, empathetic, and decent improviser who is not psychotic will learn a lot pretty early on about *not* exhibiting this type of truly selfish behavior in his improvisation, and so his fears of being "that person" in an audition are probably unfounded. He probably won't wreck or bulldoze the scene because he already knows better. Instead, he will support the reality of the scene and hold it together.

At the same time, the fear of that type of selfishness could swing a conscientious improviser the other way. The desire to support and to not be selfish may render her immobile, and she will end up doing nothing of value in the audition or show. I invite you to really consider the difference in the way of thinking that I am advocating.

Getting a laugh requires aggressive specificity, so good improvisation requires the ability to play the scene and yet find something wicked, ironic, hateful, extremely playful, or at least delightfully surprising in the context of the scene. Aggressive specificity—that's where the laughs lay, and that's where the thinking needs to be. Because, unless the essence of the scene is the rare case of purposefully being just nice and vague, then "vague" is usually a by-product of fear or the need to merely accommodate others in the scene. "Vague," without it being an aggressive choice, isn't funny. "Vague" is, well, vague.

Specificity from the absolute relentless point of view of the improviser's emotion, character, or state of mind is where the funny lies. The courage to get that quality of playful aggressive specificity and that particular somewhat cynical and confident way of looking at improvisation is much different than the accommodating, "make your partner look good and do good work" approach. The latter is passive and purely reactive improvisation. Being nice isn't actually nice to either your partner or yourself.

When will you give yourself permission to be funny in improvisation without fear of looking selfish or messing up a scene? Think of someone you truly admire in improvisation. I'll bet they make you laugh. Do they annihilate every scene they do and run all over their partner in order to get those laughs? I'll bet they don't. The people that I admire in improvisation make me laugh and don't destroy a single scene. They approach the stage with the expectation of the audience's laughter. They certainly aren't thinking, "I just want to go along, support, and get through this."

I use the word "aggressive" often. It is not an invitation to be loud and boisterous. It is an invitation to think aggressively. The type of thinking I am asking you to consider is not a "loud" way of thinking. It is quiet, knowing, cynical, and confident.

It is okay to want laughs.

It is okay.

It is okay to be funny.

9

SCENIC VARIETY

I'VE TALKED ABOUT styles. I've talked about being funny. Now I'd like to talk about variety.

This chapter is the culmination of some things I've introduced in *Improvise. Scene from the Inside Out* and discussed a bit thus far in this book. I wish to go into greater depth in regard to scenic variety. I also want to create a segue into the idea of editing in long form improvisation. Creating scenic variety and editing work in concert, for much happens simultaneously and everything influences everything else.

I consider scenic variety an extremely impactful and simple way of instantly improving the entertainment entity that is long form improvisation. Along the way, it is an approach that will help the individual find more power in improvising his scene. If I could give only one gift to all the players and all the audiences of long form improvisation, it would be this chapter on variety.

I mentioned a couple of chapters ago that in order to subscribe to my way of looking at long form, one must acknowledge that long form is an entertainment product that is performed, as opposed to a process that is merely explored. This chapter lives under that context, as well.

When I direct sketch comedy, there are, of course, many things that are important to me: how funny it is, its political relevance, the cast balance, etc. Of all the things I spend my time on as a director of sketch comedy, the one that I give the most thought to is the idea of variety. I want the show to have a lot of it. Here is an extensive, yet incomplete, list of aspects of variety that I spend hours and hours considering when I am constructing a sketch comedy running order.

- Social/political content
- Stage time for each actor
- Gender balance
- Wordy vs. physical scenes
- Presentational vs. interpersonal scenes
- Number of two-person relationship scenes
- Number of chairs in a scene
- Props vs. no props
- Costumes vs. no costumes
- Sitting vs. standing
- Different eras
- Different genres
- Quantity and styles of music
- Audience involvement
- Blocking, transitions, and blackouts

The list goes on. These things are not in perfect harmony in every sketch show I direct, but rather are tools to draw from in order to maximize the variety in the show. Sketch comedy provides the opportunity to constantly surprise the audience with disparate contexts. It is a shame when there's a lack of variety, for it's the key to letting the audience enjoy a full spectrum show with twists and pulls and tugs that place them in a whirlwind of different energies. Finding this variety is often a left-brain orchestrated event, but it can be constructed carefully and strategically beforehand. I know that the more I attend to the variety in a show, the more I can keep the audience interested, delighted, and engaged, punching the show up and delivering great momentum and more laughs. The spice of life.

For a game-based or short form improvisation show, there is also certainly room to create variety. In this genre, we learn that certain games, like Questions (each exchange must be a question or the player is "buzzed out" by the audience and replaced), are pretty good to open a show. Right after that, we probably wouldn't want another big group game, like a Madrigal or Entrances and Exits, because we want a different energy in order to create variety for the audience. Perhaps we put in a two-person Option scene or a First Line Last Line improvised scenic game—something scenic, something with a little weight or gravity. Building up to an Improvised Mini-musical or Sing-it! halfway through the show isn't an accident, but rather a purposeful running order set to create that refreshing element of variety at that point. Similarly, it isn't an accident that Freeze Tag is at the end of many improv sets. It is fast-paced, has a high hit-rate of success, and has a great variety of short scenes completely built into the game. Changing the energy *is* what that game is about.

So now let's talk about long form improvisation. On the earlier list of components that I consider in creating variety in game, narrative, and sketch shows, there are a few other elements that I purposefully left off the list because I would like to explore these concepts specifically as I apply them to long form improvisation. As I go through them, I will also discuss the value of "thinking ahead of time" when improvising in long form.

Let's start with an easy idea.

VOLUME

What is volume? Is it how loud a scene is? Yes, to a degree it is, but it's really about how loud the scene is *perceived*. Our volume can fill the room we are performing in regardless of whether we are talking loudly or talking softly. So, think about the last long form show that you were in or that you watched. Did the scenes, one after another, have the same *perception* of loudness to the audience, or were they actually pretty much the same?

Using volume as our first example, I want you to imagine yourself in the back line of a long form. For simplicity sake, let's just say it's a montage—a series of unrelated scenes inspired by a single suggestion. Standing in the back, you notice that there have been two scenes in a row where people are yelling at the top of their lungs at each other. This does happen. People sometimes get caught up in the fervor and excitement of performing, and that very often turns into a repetition of yelling from scene to scene. During the second scene of yelling, you decide to initiate an edit of the next scene, and you create a soft, frail voice, and your partner responds in kind. The value of this move at this point may be obvious. It has created respite from all the yelling for the audience.

So is this cheating since you first must have had the preconceived notion that you were going to talk softly before you executed that move? Was it wrong thinking ahead like that? Or was it just the thing to do in order to create variety for the audience? I would say the latter. Loud can be pounding like a hammer, and once an improviser starts screaming, it becomes contagious. The relief and variety a contrast provides is really appreciated by the audience and the show.

STAGE PICTURE

It's not often talked about in long form, but it's certainly given a whole hell of a lot of attention in theatre and sketch comedy. The term "stage picture" refers to where people are onstage. In any play or musical, you wouldn't want to stage five two-person scenes dead center and a little downstage unless there was a really good reason for it. It would lack visual variety and become boring. In sketch, I wouldn't put five two-person scenes back to back anyway, let alone dead center downstage. It would become noticeably obnoxious and tedious. In long form, however, we think nothing of it. I have seen *many* a long form show where this is exactly what we see, five two-person scenes standing dead center a foot and a half apart from each other, talking. There is *no* variety of stage picture or physical score (what people are physically doing) in the long form.

But what would happen to the show if, after the second scene in the same location, a player thinks, "There have now been two scenes in a row standing center stage, so I think I'm going to go downstage right and kneel to start my scene"? Did this player mess up by executing a preconceived idea, or did he make a really good move for the show instead? Once again, I would say good move.

If you think about stage picture, it is not only considering upstage or downstage, stage right or stage left. It is playing with vertical space, as well. It is perching on a ledge, passing through a doorway, or crouching on the ground. It is adding variety to the picture that the audience sees. The stage picture. It is not two people standing center a shoulder-width apart, talking and talking scene after scene after scene. If you choose to make a move to give variety to the stage picture, you, as a performer, have put on a directing hat while doing the show by noticing what the show *needs* and affecting it. Doing this is a necessary aspect of performing improvisation.

EMOTION

You are in the back line and notice that two scenes in a row are angry. Again, this is not an uncommon emotional tone for an improv scene. You decide that you want to create a "happy" declaration in the next scene. Relief for the audience, for sure.

Once again, I do *not* view this pre-thinking as cheating. Instead, I see this as responsible, professional improvisers attending to the energy of their show and constantly making it better and better by adding surprise and variety to the improvisational experience.

At this point, let's take a look at what this *type* of pre-thinking is doing to the improviser. An improviser is always thinking something while in the back line; he can't help it. Otherwise he would be dead. In long form, quite often, he is thinking about things like:

> *Okay, what am I going to do? What am I going to say next?*
> *Okay, what was the suggestion? How can I tie that back?*
> *I mustn't look at the audience. Crap, I just looked at the audience.*
> *What is this scene about? I wasn't listening.*
> *Okay, I'm going to edit... Ugh, I didn't edit.*

These types of thoughts are filtered through the improviser's *own* desires, insecurity, self-judgment, or the need to act or say something. Rarely is a long form improviser thinking about how to improve the show by providing variety and building on it.

The type of thinking I suggest takes care of both. Thinking of an element to support the variety in the show provides the improviser with a tool or roadmap to launch a scene, and it also attends to the quality of the show that they are in, all at the very same time.

Besides helping the improviser, this approach is exciting for the performer, as well. Oftentimes the patterns a show falls into are based on the performers' personal styles. If a pattern appears and it is a common choice of the performer in the back line, thinking about variety in this way invites her to execute an energy that is unfamiliar to her or create a character who wouldn't normally occur to her. Is this good? Hell yes, it is. It's scary, perhaps, but it places the improviser in her own land of variety and challenges her to stretch to an area that is unsafe and dangerous for her in a great way. The audience gets to see her discover this energy as she discovers it herself.

With variety a focus of the performer's thoughts, everyone— performer and audience—is living in fearless, exciting discovery, *and* the show is attended to. In this way of improvising long form, the player is also becoming his own teacher and director at the very same time.

So let's get back to our consideration of elements to attend to in order to create scenic variety.

RHYTHM

My favorite. This is the one I spend the most time on when directing. What is rhythm? Watch a scene and start tapping a pencil. The rhythm will come to you. Every scene has a rhythm, a pace, a speed, a beat to it.

The greatest way to create a variety of energy in a show is to affect its rhythm. Seri..ous...ly.. Rhythm is......... every...thing.

When I look at a sketch running order or the list of scenes in a show, I go through a mental rendering of the show and tap out the rhythms of scenes, songs, and blackouts. I also do the same thing while I am watching the show. I want to get the beat of those scenes in me, so I can arrange the running order so that it has a variety of rhythm and builds. This constant change-up is what keeps an audience on their toes. It keeps them guessing, jolts them into new feelings and realities, and catches them off guard in a great way. Rhythm is something that humans get accustomed to quite quickly without thinking about it, so if the mind and body of an audience member becomes accustomed to a particular rhythm, it can become lulling, and not in a good way.

The best way to create a really boring show is to pay absolutely no attention to affecting the rhythm of it.

The show was monotone.
It was predictable.
It was, like, the same scene over and over.

These are things that audience members say when they are describing boring ensemble comedy shows. These are shows that didn't attend to their rhythm, probably among other things.

Every single long form has a rhythm. Sometimes it is an amazing pace, with some fast scenes and some scenes where it rests and takes its time developing. It might pick up into a fast-paced group thing and then shoot over to a very weighty monologue. What a delight when this type of long form happens. In a show like this, everyone is playing around, having fun, and getting laughs. At the end it comes together, and it is great.

Sometimes, however, long forms have boring rhythms. I know because I've seen long forms with boring rhythms 1,298,453 times. As far as rhythm goes, it's the same show over and over. The same long form with the same rhythm. It could be in Chicago, Los Angeles, San Francisco, New York, Toronto, or Paris. I've seen that long form show in all of those places. It's the same show wherever it is. (I'll bet if they had long form on Neptune, which I'm sure they actually do, it would be the same.)

For example, perhaps the show starts with a Word Association on the theme "money." People start saying words and walking around with their heads down.

> *Money. (Long pause.)*
> *Currency. (Pause.)*
> *Yen. (Pause.)*
> *Ruble. (Long pause.)*
> *In God we trust! (Pause.)*
> *You can't take it with you. (Extra long pause.)*
> *Euro. (Pause.)*
> *Exchange rate. (Long pause.)*
> *Bank note. (Long pause.)*
> *Read the note. Put the money in the bag! (Pause.)*
> *You've got it in the bag! (Extra long pause.)*
> *I.R.A.*
> *I.R.S. (Pause.)*
> *I.O.U. (Pause.)*
> *Registered check. (Long pause.)*
> *Cash register.*
> *Ching ching! (Pause. The players start looking at each other.)*
> *Ching ching. (Pause.)*
> *Ching ching. (Everyone pipes in now.)*
> *Ching ching, ching ching. (The players begin snapping.)*
> *Ching ching. (Snap.) Ching ching. (Snap.) Ching ching. (Snap.)*

This builds and finally an improviser crosses downstage in a Sweep Edit, and the cast slowly assembles in the back line. Another actor joins the cast member onstage. They look at each other. The first is creating a pen and paper with object work. The other follows suit and starts filing papers.

IMPROVISER A: *(Seven-second pause.)* Hey…

IMPROVISER B: Hey. *(Long pause.)*

IMPROVISER A: Did you get those Jansen reports? *(Pause.)*

IMPROVISER B: Yeah. *(Long pause.)* They are right here. *(Pause.)*

I won't go on. The rhythm of this has been established. All of the pauses in a long form, like the ones represented above, are usually "thinking time" for the improviser. They are thinking between words and lines, so they aren't aware of the pauses because they are busily engaged in the act of thinking. The audience is aware of them, of course, but they don't really understand what is going on. They may just have the feeling of "What's happening? Why don't they *do* something?"

This long form is "in its head." Thinking, measurement, and a bit of fear are guiding it and informing its *rhythm*. And the rhythm it is establishing as a result of all of this is *boring*. Chalk it up to "playing slow" if you want, but it *is* boring. Ninety-five percent of the time, weighty pauses between events or dialogue in improvisation are the result of fear and thinking, not a consequence of powerful silent choice. Watching people think about what they might say someday is the opposite of interesting.

I chose for this example two culprits of a boring rhythm, as well. The Word Association opener has a notoriously slow rhythm, and Sweep Edits are culprits because their silence often resets the energy of a long form in a boring way. It doesn't have to, but it often does.

The above example would feel monotonous to the audience. The players have been seduced by the all-too-common rhythm of a group of people who are thinking and carefully approaching every moment in a safe, guarded way, as opposed to playing with wild, fearless abandon in a whirlwind of rhythms and other tools that create a variety of energies on the stage.

So what is the remedy, you may ask, to launching into a half hour of molasses? This is one area where a good, energetic opener is ideal. Again, openers set the tone and ultimately the rhythm of the entire show, so a dynamic opener will not only inform the rhythm, but create the context in which a variety of rhythms will be accepted and invited into the performance. If achieved in the opener, then a lot of rhythmic variety will naturally occur throughout the show out of a sense of great play.

Even if the opener isn't successful in establishing a healthy energy, rhythmic variety can still be achieved in the same way as the other elements mentioned before—through choice.

If you are in the back line, make it your job to ensure that no two scenes carry the same rhythm. If the scene you are watching is a slower-paced scene, change it up and bring some speed. Now! Or if the scene is a huge cacophony of energy and build, slow it down with a weightier and more purposeful initiation with your scene partner. Choose to give the show a variety of rhythms from scene to scene. Your audience will appreciate it, as will your fellow players. Putting a slower scene after a huge rise of kinetic energy in a long form is akin to putting a two-person relationship scene after a high-energy opener in a sketch comedy show. It works because of the variety of energy in its rhythm. A high-paced scene or opener gives permission for a slower scene to take place next. A big fast group song gives greater permission for a character monologue in isolated light. By rhythm alone, the slower scene is protected under the context of the faster material. Scenic rhythm allows permission and protection everywhere.

It's often hard and may even feel against the grain to *choose* to change the rhythm of a long form show, particularly if it gets into a measured or thinky rhythm, but the invitation is to *do it anyway.* Change it up right now.

If an entire ensemble can approach a show with this in mind, then instead of having each cast member in the back line constantly thinking about what *he* is going to do or not do and half listening to the scene in progress, they are all fully listening in an attempt to affect the elements of the show with great variety and surprise. And instead of latching on to an idea they'll want to force, they'll have a positive, non-restrictive focus that will give each improviser a little something to start.

Rhythm also offers another great opportunity for individual improvisers. Each of us has a natural and ingrained rhythm in our own life. When a person improvises, that natural rhythm is difficult to shake. But if a player is constantly trying to change up the rhythm to accommodate the variety of the show, then she will invariably initiate a rhythm that would not normally occur to her. It puts the improviser into a great world of welcome uncertainty.

Rhythm is the thing that influences character most. If affects the body, for sure, but also the quality and timbre of one's voice. By approaching long form with the goal of rhythmic variety, the opportunity arises for improvisers to explore different characters and energies and really stretch themselves.

LENGTH OF SCENES

Married to rhythm, the length of scenes is another thing that is very, very consistent in a very, very boring show.

If every scene is the same length, this pattern begins to get predictable and tedious. It's often difficult to vary the length of scenes in long form, because quite often the structure of the form itself will inform the length. In a Harold, for example, it seems as if we need about the same amount of time in the second round of scenes as in the first round in order to establish for the audience that there has been a time jump. The third round then usually follows the pattern and takes the same amount of time. But does it need to? If the first and second scenes properly set the context of the scene and the form, then why couldn't the third scene be two lines? It can, and it would be highly refreshing, but we often just don't think that way. We think instead, "Okay, now it's their turn to improvise for x-amount of time like we all have been doing," or "This seems like the appropriate amount of time that is allotted for scenes in this form," or "That's how long the scenes have been going in this show." It's against the grain, as I mentioned before, but my invitation would be to bravely edit that last scene and get the hell out.

Disrupt scene-length sameness by creating a new pattern of not having a pattern for scene length. Imagine a show with a few longer scenes, and then, seemingly out of nowhere, there are seven scenes that edit after about five seconds each, then a longer scene, and then a really short cast scene leading into a weighty monologue. This type of format not only provides content variety, but variety in the length of the content. Including a section of very quick scenes acts in the same way blackouts do in a sketch show. A blackout is a very short bit, usually three to five lines, where the purpose is to set up the premise and then quickly find the hook or joke in it. Blackouts are valuable in creating short bursts of quick energy and, well, more variety. Short scenes in long form take on the same valuable energy if the cast is courageous enough to edit them.

To approach a long form with variety in mind takes a collective agreement from the ensemble and plenty of practice. In a committed group of improvisers, it's a shift in thinking that can emerge very quickly and in a very powerful way.

EXERCISE

In a rehearsal with your ensemble, create a montage of scenes that aren't necessarily connected. Choose one of the elements from my list to start with, like emotion.

As you progress through the short scenes in the montage, make sure that no two scenes have the same emotional tone. Change the emotion from scene to scene. It doesn't matter if the two people editing have the same emotion themselves, as long as neither of them uses any emotion from the previous scenes.

After doing a bunch of scenes focusing on emotion, then shift to one of the other elements, like stage picture. Ensure that no two scenes in a row carry the same stage picture. Do a bunch of scenes that are everywhere onstage. Find variety in your rehearsal space.

Once you've worked with this element for a bit, change it again. The order of the elements doesn't really matter at all. It's the mindset of creating variety that is the power behind this exercise.

The elements I've discussed in this chapter are not the only fundamentals that can be used to add variety to a show, they're just the ones I consider most important. There are many more components that can make a difference, including the ones I mentioned in the sketch comedy list at the beginning of this chapter. And don't be limited to my lists alone. There are plenty of other qualities to play around with, as well. (For instance, I just thought of "status." The scenes could toggle from low status to high status to mixed status.) It doesn't matter what elements you chose to play around with, just that you are focusing on adding variety to the show.

Approaching a show with variety in mind alleviates the pain of constantly thinking, "What am I going to do? What just happened? What are they doing? What was the suggestion?" Instead, it puts the brain in a more functional, playful, and manageable place. The show is attended to, and each player has a solid support system for his individual creativity.

When focusing on variety, there is often a fear of losing other types of thinking that many people find essential in long form, like a callback opportunity, an element of connectivity for a time jump, or a tag-out option. In truth, those things are still there, but they are hopefully filtered through the even greater need to first and foremost create an entertaining show. Those elements will certainly not be lost or forgotten, but will lightly coexist with the elements of variety. If variety is attended to, those choices will be enhanced because they are filtered through the state of being you have created for yourself in approaching the next scene.

Finally, you may also fear that adhering to variety threatens your ensemble's identity. If every group does this, then yours won't stand out. To this I say that I am not pitching a particular form, but instead pitching a valuable tool to execute in any form. You've actually seen these exercises utilized in shows, either by choice or by accident in the long forms you have witnessed. You may simply remember them as "great shows."

10
THINKING AHEAD

LET'S HAVE A more in-depth conversation about preconceiving thoughts backstage or in the back line in improvisation. In the chapter on suggestions, I promised I would try to sell you on the idea that "thinking ahead" is not only okay, but can be an extremely valuable tool for yourself and for the show in which you are performing. In the last chapter about scenic variety, I went further to suggest that thinking ahead is not only an extremely valuable tool, but also how you be a responsible and professional improviser.

Every single person I have respected as an improviser has had a thought in the back line or backstage and then done something onstage based on what they thought about. Every single person. Even if the thought was just "I'm thinking about something. No! I don't want to be thinking of something. Erase, erase! Here I go," it was still thinking of something and creating an action based on what they were thinking about, in this case the avoidance of whatever that something was.

The reason this is true is because we are alive. We are unable to stop thinking. We are not zombies. We must think all of the time, and as improvisers, we often forget that. When we say, "I need to get out of my head," we are not saying that we need to stop all brain function for the duration of the improvisational experience. No, we are speaking of avoiding a particular *way* of thinking that is self-analyzing and prohibitive to play.

So if we are always thinking anyway, how about embracing the idea of thinking in a way that can be used to our advantage when we play? Why not? I've already mentioned some of the reasons we do not feel right thinking ahead of time. To review, let me list them here:

1. We don't want to create overburdened exposition that forces our partner into an impossible scenario.

2. We don't want to contrive a first line that may not fit a partner's suggestion.

3. We don't want to be caught trying to execute a funny line.

4. We don't want to cheat or feel as if it isn't pure improvisation.

Now, I agree with all of these reasons, especially the first three, but I really want to take a closer look at the last one: the feeling that our improvisation has less integrity or that we are cheating if we think of something beforehand.

Yes, I can understand why people would feel this way. But when we fear breaking the creed of improvisation (that we are making it up on the spot, pure and true), what we are really thinking about is content—the actual words. It is coming up with the actual words ahead of time that we are afraid of, and we're right to be. That *would* desecrate the integrity of the work. But that's the content, the script of what we are saying. To think of that in advance would breech our unspoken agreement with the audience—that we will make up the words as fast as they enter our brain, on the spot, right now. Creating the words ahead of time would be cheating. And indeed, the first three reasons I list above have to do with content. However, I don't believe it's cheating to preconceive "something," even though I agree it's wrong to think of the actual words.

Since we are alive and think of things no matter what, why not think of things in a liberating and empowering way? Since an ensemble of individuals is going to be thinking of stuff, I would rather they think of things and act upon things that actually support the success of show they are in. Let's take a look at *how* we can think of different things.

If you remember, in my chapter on scenic variety, I discussed the scenario of an improviser who notices a couple of angry scenes in a row and decides to create a happy, soft character when he edits. Beyond believing this is not cheating, I believe it is responsible and professional, since he is conscientiously shaping the show. His desire to create a happy, soft character is a style choice and has nothing to do with the actual words. Nothing about this choice would limit his partner or come off as contrived.

Furthermore, if he did at this point think of a couple of actual words like "the bunnies are pretty" to start his scene, it would be harmless because these words are fueled by the desire to shift style to lend variety to the piece, not to invoke a response. These, again, would not limit the natural development of the scene.

Let's look at it in another, more personal way. Let's say that lately, in every scene I improvise, I seem to lead first with my head, then my fingertips twiddle together while I'm talking, and I end up clasping my hands. (This is a Mick real-life improv example. I actually do it, and I hate it.) I lead with my head because I think too much, of course, and my fingertips, an expression of thinking, won't stop moving until I clasp my hands together in the ultimate announcement that I am in my head. So, let's say I decide in the back line that I'm going to do my next scene leading with my stomach, and I let that energy or association inspire a character and/or voice. I do it, and although it's scary, there I am improvising some character based on that thought. Did I cheat? No. Actually, the *lack* of this self-realization would be cheating. If I did not think about breaking this harmful pattern, I would be cheating myself by not actualizing growth. That's the crime. "Leading with your stomach" is not going to mess up anyone in the scene. Quite the contrary. It is making a powerful choice that has nothing to do with plot, premise, or even the content of the scene, and everything to do with stretching out and challenging me. Improvisation is an art form that invites us to say or do anything we want. Why not accept it as an invitation for personal growth as an actor and an improviser?

So let's go back to the bunny example and embellish on the fact that it actually can be fine to think of content ahead of time. It is *how* you do it that is the difference between a responsible, professional choice and a selfish, unprofessional behavior.

For example, if I suggest starting with the word "you," is it okay? It is content, actual words, but it alone is not attempting to steer the scene anywhere. It's a word that I suggest using as a content initiation if your improvisation seems disconnected lately, and you would like to declare a choice that will instantly create the idea of relationship with your partner onstage.

Another example of how you might think of something ahead of time is starting a scene by saying something you know a lot about. Does this preconceived content choice, the idea of starting with some topic about which you're actually knowledgeable, destroy the scene? Probably not, especially if your scene partner doesn't question or respond with incompetence to such specific content choices. It is a valuable tool to launch an honest, smart scene, and it allows for individual artistic expression in improvisation.

The content choices I have mentioned thus far are born either from style choice in the first example or from other shades of content choices based on personal growth or plain desire. None of them are plot- or exposition-specific, nor do they suggest following a futile path of unrealized and forced beats. They are just a starting move, to be attended to, readily dismissed, or adjusted as needed. So some preconceived content choices are fine, depending on how they are executed.

Let's explore a bit more conceptually. We've talked about variety and content for both individual growth and as an expression of self. How about a preconceived thought of playing a character that is really scary or impossible for you? This is another area of personal growth that will affect the scene but is not too heavy. Let's say you are afraid of an Irish accent as a character choice (again, me for real). So you say to yourself, "Tonight I'm going to do an Irish girl in the Living Room form." In this, I would invite you to focus on the idea of creating a context for something that scares you or that you are unsure of and then notice how that actually gives you control of it and provides a confident structure from which to play that scary thing. Preconceived ideas such as these give you a first move, if not an entire roadmap, in the scene, while creating the strong declaration that you are going to do something that scares you tonight. This actually allows you to gain power over the idea that frightens you and stretch yourself out with a tangible concept that you can bring to action. With this outlook, the chances of toppling into a powerful energy is far greater than if left to your own non-declarative devices of merely being afraid.

The same could be achieved with characters who you hate. If you were to say, "In this improvised Soap Opera tonight, I am going to play an over-the-top gay character, because I hate when people play gay people that way!" You may actually discover that this gives you permission to go there, and you would probably find that your gay character isn't that awful stereotype you were imagining, because it's actually *you* doing it and *you* are protecting it a lot more and making it a lot smarter than those who have no strong opinion about how it violates the idea of gay people. Anyway, this isn't cheating, either. Like characters who scare you, this declaration and thinking gives you greater ownership over something that confronts you in a different way.

What if you were to say, "Okay, in this scene I am going to go out there and have nothing in mind to do at all?" You say to yourself, "I am going to find a character from the first little thing that happens and then just start talking." This would be you once again making a strong choice that in this go-round of improvisation, you are going to strike or cut anything you have from your mind and improvise purely from what happens in the beginning of the scene. In other words, you are making a strong choice to go out there with nothing. This is the type of improvisation that we perceive as having the greatest integrity, that we deem pure and respectable. The difference that I am suggesting, though, is that in thinking this thought, I am creating ownership of the concept by literally declaring that I am going to think of nothing. I further encourage you to think of it as "making a game" of thinking of nothing, because this approach empowers play, lessens the importance, and adds incentive to a playable construct.

This is different than the thought, "I'm not gonna think ahead. I'm just gonna see what happens." This way of thinking has less power. It is reactive, based on an ideal, and is false, because this person *will* think of something. Thinking the thought, "In this scene, I'm going to notice the first thing and just go" is a hell of a lot different than, "I'm going to try to merely make up stuff without thinking." Making it a singular, thought-packaged event allows propriety of the "not knowing" and allows you to enter it with choice, power, and confidence.

The last constructive piece of advice on thinking ahead I can offer you is just the reminder to lightly give yourself permission to be funny.

That's my sales pitch. The end.

11
EDITING

I PREFER TO think of editing as an *opportunity* in long form improvisation. You may say, "Of course it is an opportunity. It's an opportunity to cut a scene and improvise. It's an opportunity to move the show along. It's an opportunity to stop scenes that are boring or running too long." And I would agree with all of that. By the end of this chapter, however, I hope that you'll think of edits on an even broader scale.

But first, I should visit a more basic introduction to editing, what it is and so forth, to ensure that we are on the same page. I've spoken some about editing already in my discussions of openers and back lines. Let's look at what editing really is and some different ways to approach edits.

An edit is ending the scene that is happening now and starting another. Couldn't be more simple.

There are a lot of different ways to do this. One obvious way to edit a scene is with lights. When the lights go out—that is, a blackout—the scene is over and a new one begins. This works particularly well when the form dictates that the other actors are backstage, which we talked about before. How about when people are all onstage? There are a bunch of ways to edit there, as well. One is the physical edit where a player enters the playing space from backstage or the back line, focusing away from the scene happening now and instead starting a new scene at another point onstage. The Sweep Edit I discussed before is this type of edit. An actor travels downstage and then either moves stage right or left, thereby "sweeping" the current scene away and starting another. There are other derivations of a physical edit, some of which we will discuss in a short bit.

There are also sound edits. Recalling a sound from before or introducing a new sound, either vocal or percussive, can be another way to alert the current scene that a player is going to initiate an edit. Some forms call for a more formal sound edit, like a needle drop (a short sample of music piped in quickly through the sound system) or a bell, like we often use in the game Take That Back.

Then, of course, there is a verbal edit, where dialogue becomes the indicator that a new scene, song, or monologue is now going to begin.

Of all of these, the physical edits are the most common in long form. Hopefully, a player will initiate a physical move downstage to edit on a laugh in the current scene, or at least at a point of rest or resolve. In a halfway decent ensemble, another player will nearly immediately join the player who makes the edit. The physical move, often made in silence, resets the scene and brings the show back to a neutral playing energy from which a new scene can begin. The Sweep Edit, with its travel time, resets the scene even more, literally wiping away the previous scene and introducing a new energy. The Sweep Edit also has an important rhythm that I'm not sure I can replicate here. It is the rhythm of feet going "STEP… STEP… STep, Step, step" in a sort of skip/walk on the cross downstage to wipe the scene away. The reason I went from all caps to lower case is to illustrate the volume of these footsteps as they cross. The footsteps fading in volume enhances the idea of resetting the scene. Quite often with many physical edit choices, and particularly the Sweep Edit, there is a time of brief silence onstage, usually accompanied by physical business, before the dialogue begins. It is a rest, or "breather," as a new scene starts to build.

This is a bit different from a sound edit or a verbal edit, where the new initiation cuts directly into the scene and simultaneously starts a new thing, whether a monologue, song, or scene. A dialogue edit literally starts a new scene *as* it is editing the previous one.

Any of these long form edits are absolutely fine to execute, as long as it properly alerts the current scene that it is being cut and clearly transitions to a new experience on the stage.

Let's look a bit closer at light edits, physical edits, and verbal edits.

LIGHT EDITS

Light edits are a study and a skill set all their own. From having a designated lighting person or stage manager to having the performers themselves take turns in the light booth, I have directed and performed in many shows where the lights are the edits. The upside to performing with lights as your edits is that, as a performer, you don't *have* to worry about the edit. It just happens, so you can improvise your ass off and not have to worry about being cut by another player or creating a soft out for your own scene. You just keep going until the lights go out.

The downside to light edits is that you don't *get* to worry about the edit. The show's edits are completely in the hands of another, and the improvisers have no control. This could most definitely affect the show's momentum and create a risk as to whether the edits are executed at the best time. Since it does, however, alleviate the burden of the edit from the players, which allows a different type of freedom in playing, I have at times constructed a "mixed bag," where the lights can dictate an edit or a player may edit by saying the word "scene." (Not preferred, but sometimes it may be necessary for whatever reason.)

By the way, pulling lights (controlling the lights) for an improvisation show is no easy task. If you do long form and have never pulled lights for improv and yet you have an opinion about the way someone else does it, then first of all, well, fuck you. Pulling lights for improvisation is hard. You never know when to pull the trigger, that is to say, blackout the lights. You sit in the light booth with your finger on the switch, and like in the game Freeze Tag, where you're looking for that one body position when you can yell "freeze" but it never seems to come, so are the moments in improvisation when you want to pull the lights. You wait for just the right time, and it never seems to come. It screws with your mind, because you don't want to be rude and interrupt the scene that your friends are in, but you also don't want to be rude and burn, or let go too long, the scene that your friends are in. You want to take it out at just the right spot. In a great, fast-paced show, the lights are easier. The laughs are coming fast and there are great builds and tremendous opportunities to pull a blackout. In slower shows, though, it becomes harder and harder to find that moment to pull the trigger. These scenes search for themselves with few laughs and no turn or resolve to indicate the scene's beat has concluded. It's a dance.

I recommend that *every* person who performs long form get on a light board and pull the lights for a series of improvised scenes at least once, even if just for ten minutes. Everyone would learn a lot. I recommend an entire rehearsal where this and only this happens with people rotating in and out on the lights. It not only helps you become better at editing with lights, but also at editing in general. The idea of editing gets in your body more when the lights go out as a result of a physical switch that you trigger. Doing this exercise also creates empathy for the stage manager because, as I said, doing lights for improv ain't easy.

PHYSICAL EDITS

A physical edit is great because it clearly resets the scene. After a great build, perhaps, with wonderful energy and laughs, etc., a physical edit restores decorum in the show and lets it breathe. It separates the last scene, monologue, game, or song with a feeling of, "Okay, that was that. Now let's all sit back and experience this new thing." This is all lovely and good. It creates rests and breaks in the show, and if the show has a great rhythm or pace, this is both quite welcome and beneficial.

The downside to physical edits in long form is *also* that they reset the scene—and most often to silence. These rests can be a welcome break and let the show breathe, but they can also be deadly silent traps, like the ones we discussed in regard to openers. Once again, it all depends on the *thinking* of the improvisers. Experienced improvisers who are in the middle of a great show can come out, go to their environment after a Sweep Edit, ride the energy of the last great funny scene, "hang out" in silence with a feeling of elation and presence, and maintain their spirit of play before starting a new scene. And others... well, maybe they are not feeling that wave of momentum and success. Perhaps they are thinking something different like, "This sucks. What am I doing? I don't know what I am going to say or do. Kill me now!"

It all depends.

Silence can be a threatening force to improvisers. It can either be welcome, lovely, and grounding, or the biggest fear-invoking presence in the world.

When discussing openers and the back line, I mentioned the reality that the more you wait, the more you will wait, because the momentum of the opener and thus the entire show is affected. It is exactly the same with physical silent edits between scenes. If they get into that repetitive silent rhythm, it is hard to break out of it. My *strong* advice, especially for a new ensemble, is to practice *not* making physical edits your go-to edit as most ensembles do. Instead, make a silent physical edit be something that happens *only* after a great amount of energy is established and a well-placed reset of the energy would help regain focus. That being said, it's hard to do, because many of the edits that are silent and physical have nothing to do with an ensemble's choice, and everything to do with their fear and trepidation.

And the improv thinking wheel goes round and round…

If, early on, there is a collective pattern of slow, silent, physical edits, it is likely to remain that way throughout the rest of the show. That *is* the declaration.

Opener… silent edit… first scene… silent edit… second scene… silent edit…. It's nearly impossible to suddenly launch into a strong verbal edit!

The long form itself is "in its head." Again, this is probably not out of choice, but out of trepidation from the beginning that lingers and creeps into every move that everybody makes. Yes, the more you wait, the more you will wait, and the more limited your choices become. Fewer and fewer content, character, and point of view angles feel appropriate the more silent time that passes before a scene. I must say this again:

The more silent time there is onstage, the less likely one is to make a broad, strong choice with the character, words, emotion, or point of view.

Add all of these silences up—the ones after the opener, the ones before each and every scene, and the silence that inevitably happens before each line of dialogue in the long form—and that's a lot of time devoted to being okay with your audience watching you think about things in silence. Yes, I know that's a tricky way to look at it, but it is, indeed, true. The psychology behind these edits and this approach to scenes is the main reason that boring long form improvisation is boring.

Now to make matters even worse, this particular type of slow, physical edit encourages a certain way of behaving for everyone else in the long form. It influences the way other people will approach their edits. In a really good and really fun long form improvisation, there will be an edit after a great scene where someone will come out and just ride the momentum and the fun. Another player may join them immediately, so quickly perhaps that it's hard to tell who exactly made the move to edit first. Both players just seem caught up in it and are having fun, so everyone can't wait to do the next scene. They don't care, in a great way.

This is not the case with the slow, painful silent edit. Nope. There isn't that frenzy of excitement and carefree energy on the part of the people editing. There isn't that feeling of wild abandon on the part of everyone in the back line. Instead, the feeling is, "Someone just made a silent physical edit, and they are doing something onstage. I'm going to check this out and decide whether or not to join them. Yes, what are they doing? Hmmm. Yes, I think I will join them now." Point being, the careful, slow edit encourages the other ensemble members to think carefully and slowly also. So not only the edit itself is born out of caution and fear, but the decision to join the scene is also made out of caution and fear.

Talk about adding boring kindling to the fire of tedium. More waiting. More thinking. More silence.

Please do not get me wrong. Silence out of a state of powerful, playful choice is a beautiful, refreshing, and wonderful thing. Silence out of cautious, measured fear is deadly to long form improvisation, and this type of silence is much more common.

I'll come back to this in a bit and provide some remedy, but I'd like to first move on and talk about verbal edits.

VERBAL EDITS

In long form, a verbal edit is initiating a line of dialogue from backstage or the back line to begin a new scene. It can come on its own, followed by movement, or it can be done simultaneously while moving into the playing space. For example, someone from the back line makes a verbal initiation while moving that is loud enough to be heard by the audience and the other players in the scene, thereby editing the current scene and allowing a new one to begin.

I'll state the downside to verbal edits first: they are often jolting, out of nowhere, and disconcerting.

The upside is that they are jolting, out of nowhere, and disconcerting. Sorry.

Verbal initiations in long form boldly declare the beginning of a scene. There is no messing around. The audience gets that a new scene is happening now, and they don't have to wait for fourteen seconds before someone has the courage to say something new. For the performer, it forces them into a vital, playful space. He has taken the plunge and toppled over the line into the scene. It isn't the stalking, slow beginning, but the fuck-it-here-we-go launch. Remember, it's the words we most fear, so just starting them is the hardest thing. A verbal edit into a scene gets the "starting" and the "fear" out of the way right away. It's also more likely for a fellow player to join the scene with more vigor and playful attack when the scene is initiated with words, as opposed to trying to figure out, understand, and then *possibly* join the physically initiated, silent scene.

Isn't it a bit weird for an improviser to start talking from the back line or while walking through another scene? Yes, I get it… but I'll take it. It is sometimes jolting, but as an audience member, I would rather catch up to the new scene than wait forever for a scene that was crept into with silence.

You may also be thinking, "Doesn't this just cause a lot of over-talking and interrupting?" Yes, it does! (But it really doesn't.) It seems like it would, and it's a common concern in rehearsals, but put it to a field test, and it evens out just fine. God forbid two people are jumping at the chance to start a scene! Believe me, it works out much more often than not.

And how about those edits that *do* come after a great funny scene with amazing energy? "Are we supposed to talk through those and not have that wonderful resting and resetting silence?" My answer to that would be, "I hope that this is the problem you have. I hope that your long form has so much vibrant energy, comedy, and momentum that to speak out loud immediately after the last great scene would be combative and inappropriate." I hope that is a real concern for you.

Ultimately, as with all of this, I am once again strongly suggesting balance and variety. If your group launches an opener that creates a furious rhythm for your long form and you have to silently go into every next scene because of the raucous energy you have created together, then awesome. If not, keep an eye on it. Your silent physical edits may be a product of your measured thinking, and it won't get any better. Just as in scenes, balance and variety is key when editing. If variety, as a choice, is front and center in an ensemble's mind when editing, then that will take precedence and will lead to more mood-appropriate and well-timed edits.

So if I, as a player, have noticed two physical edits that take their time getting to the words in the scene, then perhaps I'll make a sound edit by adding ambience after a scene that I raise in volume while moving into the next scene. Or if I notice three strong verbal edits in a row, I will choose to come out with a Sweep Edit to settle the energy and provide variety to the pace of the show. Once again, I am using edits to lend variety to the show to make it better, not just thinking of an edit as a way to get me onstage. For too many of us, an edit is a necessary utility move to get back in the performance arena, as opposed to an opportunity to create more variety and control the pace of the show.

It is important as a player to be able to read a scene and edit at an appropriate point, hopefully the end of a beat. So when *does* the beat end? When *should* you edit?

This is a common question. I can say the following with some certainty:

1. You actually kind of know when the beat ends. You have a better feel for it than you think.

2. Almost always go for a quicker edit than a longer edit as a rule of thumb. The bigger problem in long form improvisation isn't that everybody is cutting all of their scenes way too fast. The more you wait...

3. Technically, the beat ends with a transformation of point of view, a resolve, or at least a change in the scene. If you have ever been on lights for improvisation, as mentioned earlier, then scenes that sustain the same level, argue with no resolve, and remain linear with their unchanging points of view are most difficult to edit or pull the lights on.

So here's a couple of exercises that will help put this stuff together a bit. The first is a verbal editing exercise. It's all about practicing the skill set of verbal edits. Let me repeat the words "skill set." It's a decision, first of all, to even call editing a "skill set." That means it is a concept that is tangible and can be learned and improved upon. I think we kind of know that, but I don't think we declare it as such. We probably rarely have edit-only rehearsals. It's usually about the scenes, the openers, the games/group scenes, or the specific form. It is rarely about rehearsing the skill set of edit technique. Well I'm telling you, it is a skill set, and some groups are better at it than others.

Read the following exercise rather carefully.

EXERCISE

The group is going to do a bunch of very short, self-edited scenes.

The scenes are edited with words.

The scenes are two lines long.

There are absolutely no pauses between the lines in the scene.

There are absolutely no pauses between the scenes.

There are no interruptions.

So it is: Two lines. *(Edit.)* Two lines. *(Edit.)* Two lines. *(Edit.)* etc.

And... go. Do that for a while, won't you?

During this exercise, a couple of things start to happen that will need to be adjusted after a while. There usually is a good pace with this, but a lull does often come in between the scenes. Each new two-line scene takes a couple of short beats to rev up. Similarly, there is a great temptation to react a little right after the second line, which does slow down the pace a bit. Once these lulls appear, just stop and encourage the players to more strongly jump on the next scene immediately after the second line. After resuming with these adjustments, it will fly a bit better. Yes, there will be interruptions and some lulls, but it isn't really about the rightness and wrongness of hitting the exercise, it is about the powerful adjustment in the hearts and minds of the players. No longer does it matter *what* you say to edit, it is truly *that* you edit. It is about the mindset of eliminating pauses and fulfilling the desire and need to edit the scene *first*, and then caring about the content, or the words you are saying.

Once the flow of this exercise is moving nicely, you can make another adjustment to eliminate disparate responses on the second line of the scenes. Sometimes the response is too different in regard to the initiation:

IMPROVISER A: Hammers come in many sizes.

IMPROVISER B: I like mayonnaise!

Responses from Mars, so to speak. Completely unrelated. Encourage improviser B to acknowledge her partner's suggestion and make a game of how quickly she can do this with her own character or point of view. It doesn't matter whether it is out of agreement or not as long as it is acknowledged. Sometimes the word "acknowledgement" merely means lifting a word and repeating or restating it slightly in the response.

IMPROVISER A: Hammers come in many sizes.

IMPROVISER B: I hate sledge hammers!

I know these examples are a bit declarative and basic, but this exercise sometimes reflects a basic feel in the beginning, and then becomes more playful and substantive as it goes along.

Eventually, this exercise gets to the glorious point of truly not caring what you say and just having fun keeping in the game of quick edits. Players learn a bit about themselves, too. If they are continually waiting, but never editing, I would bet that behavior isn't specific to this exercise, but an indicator as to how they manage themselves in any long form or other improv experience. Perhaps they are going out too much. Or maybe they always initiate with a reference to an animal (like me). The mere volume of these short scenes highlight and magnify an improviser's overdone or destructive patterns.

EXERCISE

Here's another exercise that will help to identify the end of a beat in a scene. I said earlier that people kind of know the end of a beat more than they think. Well, I would like you to play Freeze Tag with this in mind. At this point, you must think that I am a Freeze Tag queen or something. I hate Freeze Tag. It's a drag to play, and I always dread it after a Second City improv set. I do, however, believe that it is a valuable tool for a lot of improvisation constructs, and as such, I really don't hate it as much as I just said.

So play Freeze Tag, but with a very simple honor system agreement with your group: you yell "freeze" only when the previous beat is over. "Huh? We always perform Freeze Tag with 'editing when the beat is over' in mind," you may protest. No. You don't.

In reality, you look at the waist level of the people in the scene, trying to catch something to freeze on, and then out of pure necessity, you edit the scene with or without an idea because you think too much time has gone by.

In this exercise, I'm asking you to remove the importance of two things:

1. The need to look at the body, trying to catch something to freeze on.

2. The need to be funny.

I'd like you to not care what you have in mind when you say "freeze" other than watching and listening very closely to when you feel the beat is over. That's it. That's why I say it's on the honor system. Only you really know what you're thinking, but I seriously want you to let go and try it.

You will learn a couple of things from really doing this for a while. As an ensemble, you'll see that different people have different senses as to when a scene or beat is over. Some players will learn they edit too soon, and some will let beats go on too long. All of this can be reflected upon after the exercise. This exercise may also encourage a conversation within the ensemble about what they consider a good amount of time before an edit, and this discussion could lead to a consensus, depending on the particular form.

With Freeze Tag, there are some who believe that the most effective way to play it is fast and furious, a two lines per beat, joked out explosion of scenes. Others see, or at least would like to see, Freeze Tag as a scenic exploration, where the device of changing the premise of the scene by clarifying body position is just an opportunity to inspire another long scene. Neither of these approaches are wrong. They are just different philosophies about Freeze Tag. These exact same points of view are also found in regard to the elements of long form. Some think of it as fast and furious, and others see it as a slow build. Some, like me, would like to see it as a mix of both.

A third thing that you can learn from these two exercises is that what you say in the nano-moment of not thinking, just doing, is *as effective* or often *even better* than anything you can think of beforehand. The thing you think of on the spot in Freeze Tag is just as good or just as funny as the moment you are trying to catch as you look at people's arms. Again, *that* it is edited is the most important thing when it comes to satisfying the completion of a beat and editing the scene.

This way of thinking is what will add up to a great show with great momentum, realized conclusions, turns and twists, resolves, fun, and play. Not to mention a much funnier show. The opposite approach could lead to a lot of time waiting under the guise of silent character exploration, environment, and object work.

EXERCISE

This final exercise is about creating a powerful choice, even if there is a decent amount of silence at the beginning of the scene. It's a favorite, as well.

It comes in two parts.

First, like the two-line edit exercise, I would like you to eliminate time between things, but with a twist. This exercise consists of a series of timed two-minute scenes. During a scene, each person is allowed only one sentence of dialogue each time they speak, no more. It's just two people saying only one sentence at a time, back and forth. There is no time between the lines of dialogue. There are no interruptions, and each person must talk as *fast* as they can! Seriously, talk *fast*.

I must emphasize that they are only to speak *one* sentence at a time, because people tend to get caught up in the energy of this and ramble on.

Go ahead and run this exercise focusing on just this part first. What do you get from it?

I get the following:

1. You can get a lot done in a couple of minutes if you eliminate the bullshit.

2. Once again, what you are saying as you think about it right now is just as fun as what you may have thought of beforehand.

At this point some of you may be struggling to reconcile my previous thoughts on the value of pre-thinking an idea before you improvise with the value of just saying whatever very fast with absolutely no thinking, so I want to make a quick side note and address this. It really isn't that big of a difference. Consider this approach as another pre-thought construct. It is the preconceived idea of "choosing to improvise very fast with nothing in mind." You are essentially accepting the invitation to pre-think the improv construction of improvising one line at a time without pauses and speaking very quickly. That's the game.

So, back to this exercise. In part one, you find that you can get a lot done and have as much fun saying it now as when you think about it beforehand. A lot of people also learn that they can talk a hell of a lot faster than they thought they could before.

Now, part two of this exercise is a bit weirder and definitely harder. I want you to do the same exact thing, speaking one line at a time as fast as you can, going back and forth in a scene for two minutes. The only difference now is that I want you to pause and silently count slowly to five before each of your responses.

IMPROVISER A: *(Speaks as fast as he can.)* The trains are running express at rush hour tonight.

IMPROVISER B: *(Counts very slowly in his head to five, and then responds very fast.)* I'm gonna take the Purple Line to Howard Street and then double back!

IMPROVISER A: *(Counts very slowly in his head to five, and then responds very fast.)* Yes, that's better than the bus, because I'm late for a date.

And on it goes for two minutes.

This exercise doesn't make sense, because it works against the better instinct of the brain. Usually, very fast words do not come from a place of silence, so when they do, it is a bit disconcerting. It doesn't feel right. And that's exactly why I want you to experience it. I want you to feel the difference between speaking out of an uncomfortable silence without much confidence, and the feeling of being completely okay with the silence that you *choose* to the point that you can then powerfully and confidently execute a line of dialogue. In this case, the line of dialogue is a very fast one to help launch into that feeling of self-assurance.

I want you to use this exercise to get a feeling for speaking powerfully both when you *choose* a silent edit as a matter of creating variety and when you *end up* in a silent, uncomfortable edit because you feel a bit trapped in a long form with a measured and think-filled energy. It may not feel exactly right to break out with a different kind of verbal energy, but you *can* do it, even after a five-second pause.

Let me digress for a moment and discuss why it does feel so weird to bring this dialogue out of silence.

Silence is a real thing in improvisation. It is a unit of energy. At the beginning of a scene, it is a presence that takes up space and time. With a silent declaration comes certain tendencies and limitations. As mentioned earlier, the more silence there is at the beginning of a scene, the fewer choices seem to be available to us, because a great many don't feel right. This is because prolonged silence carries with it an inferred meaning. The meaning itself has parameters, and when we speak from those inferred meanings, we want it to make sense within their parameters. For example, one logical thing to come out of silence would be the aftermath of an intense argument. Imagine two people in a very heated argument, and then there is complete silence. Imagine the tense feeling in the room. Now imagine the kind of things people might say from this kind of silent tension. The appropriate choice of things to say in this declared reality is limited. Our emotional tone is also limited, and it requires us to say words that either clarify an uncomfortable previous scenario, lighten it up to break the silent tension, or possibly even continue the adverse points of view. It would be odd for two people in a scene to linger in silence together for seventeen seconds, perhaps doing some quiet physical business, and then have one of them point up and say with elation, "The circus is coming to town!" Now I would actually love that (and part of the point of the exercise above is to make verbal initiations like this more available to your thinking), but in reality, it doesn't happen very often because it doesn't feel right with the implied meaning of the silence.

Another example of a situation to proceed out of silence would be two people who don't know each other, like in a waiting room or bus stop, perhaps exchanging glances. The only dialogue to logically come out of this silence would be words of unfamiliarity, small talk, and niceties. Again, to have one of them blurt out loudly, "The circus is coming to town!" after twenty-two seconds of glancing at each other would feel odd, though once again, I would find it refreshing. I wouldn't put my money on an improviser actually bringing that line out of that much silence, however. I would place my bets on something like, "So, the bus is late again," or "You live around here? I've never seen you at this bus stop before," or "Late for work."

The amount of possibilities open to players for initiating a scene definitely dwindle the more time is swallowed up in silence.

EXERCISE

Think "go" to yourself in your mind as if you are starting a scene. As soon as you think "go," say anything you want immediately.

(Think "Go.") The circus is coming to town.

Now do it again, but this time count to two before speaking the line.

(Think "Go... one... two.") The circus is coming to town!

Keep adding time to the silence after you think "go." You will start to feel the burn, or the uncomfortable feeling of waiting, and how it increases the inappropriateness, the importance, or the gravity of the line. The silence becomes a real, tangible piece of energy that adds weight to the line, no matter what it is.

This is akin to the phenomenon of being in a scene in silence and the ever-increasing difficulty of speaking the more "silent time" goes by. If you reach a tipping point in the scene, it will feel very wrong to speak at all, and your choices of what to say become even more limited because the choice must justify thirty-nine seconds of silence, as opposed to twelve seconds or just one second of silence. It is more difficult because the silence gains more meaning as the time increases. The choices for that line of dialogue are going to be less plentiful and definitely less playful.

This idea even extends to being the third person out in a three-person scene. These three-person scenes often start with two of the three people onstage beginning the dialogue. They get something going, and before he realizes it, the third person is stuck in a silent activity, like doing laundry or painting. The longer he waits to say something, the harder it is to say anything at all. It often gets to a point where the audience begins to wonder what that third person's function is in the scene. It becomes inappropriate for him to suddenly declare the energy or point of view created by the other two improvisers, but he eventually has to carve out *something* to say. That something often ends up being adversarial or negative toward the others' shared activity or point of view. Ultimately, silence, and the vacuous, weighty anchor that it brings to the scene, yields greater implied stakes often rooted in adversity or conflict.

Recall the previous exercise with the conscious five-second wait before speaking powerfully and confidently: it's okay to bring these words out of silence. The choices are far greater than you might think if you just have the courage to make those choices against the silence.

Bringing this all together, I would like to conclude this discussion by inviting you to take a look at editing as a thing in and of itself, just as silence is a tangible element of energy in a long form scene. Think of it almost as if editing is a whole other character or presence in your show. It is a real contextual element that can provide the show with not only momentum, but also more variety and a greater declaration of connectivity and style. I'm not necessarily talking about the content of what is actually said in the edits. I'm speaking more about the type of edits, how and when they are executed, and how they become an opportunity for pace, variety, and unity of style and context in long form.

As I said earlier, we often think of an edit as a utility move, just something to get us from scene to scene. We will cross through a scene on a laugh, engage a Sweep Edit, or perhaps orally start a scene from the other side of the stage. Most of the time, it is only about getting to the next thing based on an individual's desire to follow an idea or the feeling that the beat of the scene is over and that it needs to be cut. Both of these are certainly noble and necessary, but in my opinion merely thinking this way is often a lost opportunity.

Edits, if thought about as a whole concept, can add another exciting, enlightening, and substantial layer to long form improvisation in addition to launching an idea or sustaining momentum.

Here's an example. Let's say an ensemble is doing a montage and creates an opener based on the suggestion "birds." The players fly around making observations about Chicago from a bird's-eye view. They build the opener and then slow down and settle into the first scene about two owls in a tree. At the end of the scene, there is a Sweep Edit, and the next scene begins. It is a couple in Austin talking about the bat problem they have in the attic. There is another Sweep Edit, and the third scene is about someone being a birdbrain at work. During the scene, someone in the back line yells, "Birdbrain! Birdbrain!" and comes out to edit the scene.

Another improviser responds, "So it's done. 'Birdbrain' is the name of our band." After a bit, there is another Sweep Edit into a group scene about a flight school. This group scene escalates into a yelling match until one of the actors suddenly breaks from the group, silently travels down left, and silently starts building something. Another improviser notices and joins in silence. This transitions into parent-child scene where the child is building a model airplane in the basement.

If you didn't catch all the details of this montage, it doesn't matter. I tried to keep it simple so as not to infer any particular form that would dictate a particular type of edit. It's just a simple collection of scenes. Now let's break it down a bit.

First, let's set up a running order for this montage:

Bird's-Eye View Opener
(Settles.)
Owl Scene
(Sweep Edit.)
Bat Scene
(Sweep Edit.)
Birdbrain Scene
("Birdbrain" vocal repetition edit.)
"Birdbrain" the Band Scene
(Sweep Edit.)
Group Flight School Scene
(Silent environment edit.)
Model Airplane Scene

Let's assume the scenes in this were fine scenes, that is to say, they went just fine. They were good scenes. They were smart and fun. This keeps the scenes consistent so that we can now look at the edits.

1. Sweep Edit

2. Sweep Edit

3. Vocal Repetition Edit

4. Sweep Edit

5. Silent Environment Edit

So now I ask you, what were the edits *about*? Every scene is hopefully about something based on an observed pattern of behavior, voice, mannerism, emotion, or point of view. So what are the edits *about* in this set? Think of it in the same way that you might think of a scene. They are a declaration of a point of view, a state of mind, a game, or a behavior to be acknowledged and heightened. So what are these edits, all together taken as a character or scene, about? For example, maybe the group of edits in this montage can be defined as Sweep Edits? Well, even though the majority are Sweep Edits, they aren't all Sweep Edits, so this is not the declaration being made by these edits. Since there are three types of edits occurring here, all that can truly be said about these edits as a whole is that they end one thing and start something new. That's the only recognizable pattern or constant between these edits. "Well, of course," you might say. "What's the point?"

Let's quickly take a look at the system of editing improv games, starting with Freeze Tag. The game of Freeze Tag is edited by a player in the back line yelling "freeze," sometimes combined with a hand clap. When this occurs, the actors freeze and the player from the back line takes one of the player's exact physical positions and changes the scene.

Now let's look at Take That Back (a.k.a. New Choice, or hundreds of other names). Every time a moderator hits a bell, the actor that just spoke stops and repeats their last line in a new way. The edit is the bell.

In Entrances and Exits, an actor enters or exits the stage any time an assigned word or phrase provided by the audience is spoken. Stating an audience-suggested word or phrase prompts an entrance or an exit, and thus is the edit in this game.

Unlike long form, games often have built-in constructions that inform the style or method of editing. Whether you are pointed at by a conductor in Conducted Story or you are "buzzed out" by the audience because you failed to form a question in the game Questions, the editing method is consistent, and everyone is in on it from the performers to the lights and sound people to the audience. The editing style is often its own character and frequently helps define the game. Editing is the "game" of the game.

Most of the time in long form, the only consistency is *that* it is edited. Truly, editing is rarely paid attention to at all. And it really doesn't have to be. Long form is long enough—and often transformational, amorphous, and fluid enough—that any edit becomes okay as long as it is dictating the change in the elements of the form. As long as we know we are going from one thing to the next, it really doesn't matter how it is edited.

With that said, there are sometimes fashions or trends in long form editing that arise in different schools or cities. Even these whims, however, are not dictated by need or the form itself. The fact that the long form *is* edited is still paramount.

With this in mind, let's take a look at another running order of the bird scenes, but with different edits.

Bird's-eye View Opener
(Settles.)
Owl Scene
(A player conducts a Sweep Edit with outstretched arms flapping like a bird.)
Bat Scene
(Another Sweep Edit with flapping arms.)

Birdbrain Scene
(Another Sweep Edit with flapping arms.)
"Birdbrain" the Band Scene
(Another Sweep Edit with flapping arms.)
Group Flight School Scene
(Another Sweep Edit with flapping arms.)
Model Airplane Scene

So in this example, what is the concept of the edit about? It is boringly apparent that it is about "flapping arms." Every single edit is a player or players flying across stage like a bird to sweep the scene clean for the next scene. First thought: this might get very boring and predictable. Yes, maybe. But that's not the point right now. The point is that the edit becomes a thing, a tangible concept in and of itself inspired by the theme. This group noticed the move "flying across stage to edit" and embraced it as an element of the form.

Let's look at another quick running order. I'm going to strip the scenes of their identity so as to just look at the edits.

Opener
(Settles.)
Scene A
(A player conducts a Sweep Edit with arms flapping like a bird.)
Scene B
(A player flies across the stage with outstretched arms like an airplane.)
Scene C
(A player does another airplane, but faster and more streamlined like a jet.)
Scene D
(A player launches across the stage like a rocket.)

Scene E
(A player flies across stage like Superman.)
Scene F

Now these edits are about modes of flying represented by arm movements. The player doing the second edit chose to build on the first player's edit, thus creating a theme-related pattern that was recognized by the remaining players as an edit technique that needed to be heightened throughout. Suddenly the edits take on an identity that is far from boring.

And yet another running order:

Opener
(Settles.)
Scene A
(A player conducts a Sweep Edit with outstretched arms flapping like a bird.)
Scene B
(A player flies across the stage with outstretched arms like an airplane.)
Scene C
(A player makes a train sound and crosses the stage moving his arms like a train.)
Scene D
(A player crosses the stage as if riding a bicycle.)
Scene E
(A player moves across stage like he is operating an outboard motor on a boat.)
Scene F
(A player drives a truck, pulling the horn and honking.)

Now the edits are about different modes of transportation that are represented by arms and sound.

The focus when creating edit identities could be on recognizing and developing patterns. If the first edit has flapping arms, the pattern could even simply be arm movements, like karate chops or robot arms. The edit context does not have to be complex in order for the edits to become a definable, interesting element.

The pattern also does not need to be grounded in the physical. Here is an example of a more complex edit context based on actual dialogue. The audience suggestion for this example was "telephone."

During the opener, one of the players says, "Watson, come here. I want to see you." The opener settles and the first scene begins. One player in the back line initiates an edit by building on the line from the opener. "Watson, can you hear me? How have you been?" Another player joins him and says, "Fine. And you, Mr. Bell?" These two players then begin an entirely new scene, not based on this Watson and Bell phone call. In the next edit, two new players continue the Watson and Bell conversation before beginning another new scene, etc.

In this example, the edits themselves are a scene about a phone call between Watson and Bell. What was that call like? Does it heighten to the point of Watson wanting to get off the phone, but Bell won't wind down the call? These edits are another organic element in the show based on the audience suggestion. They are a thing, in and of themselves, created as another layer to the form.

The math of this seems a bit daunting at first, but it really isn't. It is actually quite simple. Try this exercise to get your ensemble thinking more productively about the edits.

EXERCISE

Do a series of scenes that are short and serve only to get to the edits. Focus on declaring a pattern and building on it in the edits. In one hour and twelve minutes, you will start to get a feel for how this works and how it can be adapted to fit any form.

Start with physical choices that have no sounds or words. For example, if someone shakes one hand in the air on the first edit, then all subsequent edits involve shaking two hands, then feet, then head, then bodies, for example.

When you've practiced this a few times, try it with sounds. Someone in the first edit makes a sound, then it is duplicated in the second edit, elongated in the third, and so on. Move on to words and short exchanges, until you reach the point where you are building a scene within the edits themselves.

Now, it's also possible that your edit context could be creating the most unrelated and different edits possible. This, then, becomes the inherent artistic choice for the form.

Approach your edits keeping the following list in mind:

- Choice

- Declaration

- Recognition of Pattern

- Heighten and Build the Pattern

- Enjoy Success

This way of thinking about editing brings connectivity, continuity, and theatricality to your long form creations and turns them into a more cohesive and polished entertainment product.

12
SUSTAINING A CHARACTER

WHEN IT COMES to creating and sustaining a character in an improv scene, I feel like I could write a book about it. *Improvise. Scene from the Inside Out* covers the subject in detail, so I'm not going to belabor it here. I am, however, going to emphasize some areas and provide some tips that I feel are more specific to long form improvisation than other types of improvisation.

To understand my approach to sustaining a character, you have to get where I'm coming from. Here is a brief overview of what I think about an improv scene, but to truly understand each point, I strongly suggest reading the full discussion in my other book. (If you don't, I'll seriously kill you.)

1. I believe that rules in scenic improv are overrated and that thinking about them too much will cause you to lose power in your performance.

2. I believe that at the top of an improv scene, selfishness is the greatest virtue, for the choice you strongly make to

take care of yourself is the very thing that *is* taking care of your partner.

3. I believe that we can talk about listening, finding a relationship, and supporting your partner all day long, but in the end, a point of view, character, or any other identifiable behavior, state of being, or pattern that is recognized becomes what the scene is about for you.

4. Thinking "yes, and" too much is powerless saccharin in improvisation. Aggressively and relentlessly pursuing your vision in an improv scene—even if that vision is quiet, subtle, lovely, or vulnerable—is a much more valuable and proactive way of approaching improvisation.

I'll stop there. I truly believe all of these things, and for long form improvisation, I believe them even more.

But before we discuss sustaining a character in long form, I want to visit the moment when the character is created.

In long form, this moment of creation must happen faster than in other forms, even if it appears slow. This may seem counterintuitive since, by definition, "long" implies that there is more time. In reality, there *is* more time to create many scenes and energies. Even if the long form is actually one self-contained scene, the amount of time that long form allows provides ample opportunities for multiple themes, directions, plots, backgrounds, etc. There is time in long form.

That being said, I believe that a scene in long form must establish what it is about even *earlier* and be played even *harder* than a scene lasting only two to four minutes. This is necessary to give the audience a more solid foundation that will be able to support the entire length of the scene, to provide further clarity for callback potential, and to differentiate the scene from all the other elements in the show. By this I mean other scenes, characters, games, etc.

In short, in long form, you have to get to it fast… even more.

Long form is usually the exploration of different scenes based on a single suggestion over time. So given that, do we want each element of the long form—every scene, game, group scene, song, and monologue—to meander aimlessly, "search," and "find" itself? Ironically, I don't think there is time for that. I believe that quickly finding something in the scene with singular focus is essential to the life of a long form and much more powerful. We want to get to the scene quickly, improvise our asses off, and stay focused so that the audience understands what's up in that particular scene. In this way, the improviser can truly explore a single, different idea based on the suggestion.

In other types of improvised scenes, I believe one has a little more freedom to "check the scene out" a bit. Provided that the players are in a relatively healthy head space with their scene, they may even have the luxury of taking some shots with a light point of view at the beginning, and then fishing around a bit for a greater dominant energy to latch on to. Once found, they may repeat or slightly add to something to declare its pattern and eventually evolve the "center of the scene," or what the scene is about. In these average scenes, a strong improviser can lie back a little and then pounce on an idea of his choosing.

In long form, although we often *feel* that we have more time to find a scene, we actually don't. The amount of time it takes for the audience to perceive that the actors are "fishing" or "waiting" or "trying to find something to do/say" actually decreases with long form. The audience has less tolerance for this journey, because the entire form *is* this journey. Instead, they want the improvisers to just make a choice and provide quick clarity in their scenes. It is far more interesting and refreshing for them to watch the actors latch on to anything immediately than to watch them think, wait, and look for things in every scene every time.

Even if you are playing with the idea of "slow" in mind, get to what you are playing slow fast! Either by experience, choice, or luck, this is what a good scenic improviser in long form does.

They *get to it.*

So, the first part of sustaining a character is creating something that is worth sustaining.

When approaching a scene, improvisers are afraid of losing the character later on. "Will I be able to sustain the character? Will I be able to heighten the scene?"

To this I reply, "Why be afraid of losing something that you don't even have in the first place?" This is what my friend, Bob Levitt, used to tell me when I was unsuccessfully selling vending machines to businesses. He would say, "You're afraid of losing something you don't even have in the first place... the sale!"

An improviser's fear of losing the scene/character prevents her from creating something worth losing.

What you do early on will absolutely determine how it will play out. If you have nothing to sustain or heighten because you did not immediately make a choice for yourself, recognize that choice, and establish its pattern, you are probably *not* going to magically get something later on. You have to create something remarkable right off the bat in order to heighten or play something remarkable.

Now, let's take a look at the thinking you do when approaching long form. One of the most common psych-outs in long form is that, because it is *long* form, we think that we can't sustain or heighten something for that long. First of all, it isn't that long. It really isn't.

When we think of long form, we have it in our heads that we are improvising ten- to fifteen-minute scenes. We're not. In a good long form, there is a wonderful balance of the real estate of stage time in the show, and each person's relative responsibility isn't nearly as long or great as many improvisers believe it to be. It really adds up to just a few minutes if you do the math. (I love math, you hate it.) As with many ironies in improvisation, it is the very thought of LONG form and the resulting fear that truly prevents a player from holding on to a character or sustaining the scene. Self-fulfilling prophecy.

In long form, you really only have to hold on to something for two or three minutes at a time. So, seriously, chill out.

I want to throw some words out there that long form improvisers often *don't* have in mind when they are improvising and sustaining a scene's point of view and character:

Aggressive

Passionate

Possessed

Consumed

Attack

Reinvest

Ignite

Pounce

These are emotion-driven, active ways of thinking that will fuel the fire of your creation in a long form scene. These words, and the feelings that they invoke, are often overshadowed by the calculating tendencies that accompany long form.

I say think all you want, but then attack, pounce, and ignite your performance. It is only with this fervor that you will create something worthy of holding onto in the first place. That is the key to sustaining a scene: aggressively pursuing that which you relentlessly and fearlessly created. Only then can you truly invest and reinvest in the magic of that tangible creation.

There are so many times when I have heard improvisers complain about not being able to hold on to something or sustain it in long form, and I just want to say, "Wow, you had a hard time maintaining that character that paused, thought a lot, and said things like 'Factories are fun. This is the best factory ever'? That *amazing* declaration in the scene? You couldn't hold on to the tremendous power of that tentative expositional filler at the top of the scene that was based in your fear? I can't believe it."

Perhaps it's because your choices weren't fueled by any of the attributes in my list.

A quick disclaimer about my list: I'm not suggesting loud or angry or loud and angry. You can be "passionate" about the silence in the library or "attack" being slow and bored.

It's all about committing and constantly reinvesting in your scene.

Let's say you find yourself silently sewing a sock in a scene. Here's a great opportunity to start thinking some bad, destructive thoughts like, "What am I doing?" or "Why am I doing this?" If even the slightest inkling of this type of thinking starts to creep into your mind, *reinvest* now! Reinvest in the sewing. Commit to it even *more*. Must. Sew. Sock. With. More. Commitment.

Sewing a sock is something you created. It is *there*, it is *true*, and it is *real*. Is it the funniest thing in the world? Is it an *amazing* initiation? No, it probably isn't. But it is *real*, you really did create it, and anything that you actually created is far better than anything you did not. Sewing, for that moment, is *everything*. So reinvest in the sewing. This doesn't necessarily mean do it faster or bigger, but to mentally focus completely on the sewing. It is a cadence and psychology that has you embody more commitment to that sewing, to that creation. So in a physical sense, everything becomes more specific and executed with more authority and shape and weight. You "feel" the drag of the needle more as you bring it up through the cloth, and you struggle just that little bit more to get it through the cloth. That's all you are thinking.

Now with words, reinvest in the point of view, the content, the voice, and/or the mannerisms of that character you have created. No matter how subtle the character. Does the character stutter or passionately stumble on a word?

Let's say, for example, you created a character who is slightly bored by everything. I used "slightly" and "bored" on purpose because of their subtlety. In that moment of the scene when you are about to start getting in your head, *pounce* on being even more bored. The moment you start overthinking, *jump* on rolling your eyes in a bored, distracted manner or shifting in an indifferent, passive way. Being bored is your creation, so that's all the audience cares about and that is all there is in regard to the power of the scene. They don't care about your opinion about holding on to the scene.

Constantly reinvest in your own creation. The trick is to be so consumed by what you have created that "How do I hold on to this?" can never enter your mind. By constantly recommitting and reinvesting, you can keep the demons out. You must, for a scene will not be sustained if you linger on the thought, "I must sustain this scene."

In great long form scenes that you have been in and/or watched, remaining focused in the scene is exactly what happens. But you never think about it. It's just… fun.

Having just mentioned demons, let's discuss another word from my list: "possessed."

Usually, of course, when we think of being possessed, we think about demonic possession. Possessed by the devil. So let's take a look at being possessed by the devil. How do people know that someone is possessed by the devil? Because everything they do and say is different and weird to the point that someone can only rationalize their behavior as being "possessed." Let's look at the qualities of someone who is possessed. They constantly do and say things that are of the nature of their possession. They, without really thinking about it, are constantly portraying a "possessed person."

Now let's look at long form. The audience wants to see you possessed by your character, emotion, physical mannerisms, or any other tangible declaration you have made in the scene. They are dying for you to be possessed. Did you cough once? Be possessed by coughing. Did you repeat your first line? Be possessed by the "demon of repeating things." Whatever it is—however big, little, loud, quiet, obvious, or subtle—be possessed with that energy. Want something to think about in improvisation? Think about how every sound, movement, and word can add to the possession you feel through what you've created. No room for anything else in the brain—just that! Pure, satanic possession of an idea, thought, point of view, or character. You are possessed by the energy.

The way he's acting, he must be possessed!

He must be. "To possess" means "to own." *Own* your creation. Own your creation and filter every move and word through that ownership. Besides, you can't help but do so. You're possessed.

I am going to explore one last word from my list: "attack."

Attack every line as if you are just waiting for your partner to shut up so you can speak. Yeah, listen to them, but have the energy of "Pounce! Attack!" even if there is a lapse of five seconds, like the exercise I had you do earlier with editing. No matter what, when that line comes, attack it! You just can't wait to say or do the thing that has you demonstrate more of what you are and more of what the scene is about. You can't wait. You are going to wait… but you just can't… attack!

Reinvest = Possessed = Attack. All of these concepts work in harmony. Words that have people create, recognize that creation, and then wholeheartedly pursue it until the end.

In long form improvisation, all of this comes together to form the vision for our scenes. Relentlessly realizing our ideas is the magic and joy of improvisation.

These are the scenes in long form that have relationship, clarity, realism, stupidity, tension, laughs, and meaning.

Fuck it.

13
GROUP SCENES OR GAMES

GROUP ENDEAVORS IN a long form can really suck. Sometimes they can be good. Every once in a while, they can be great. I am going to explore this topic through a series of exercises for an ensemble. With each of these exercises, I will state a goal or an issue, and then use the exercise to challenge that goal or issue. This isn't about any particular group scene or game, but rather an over-riding philosophy and approach to what we often refer to as the "group mind."

Let's start.

When it comes to group work in long form, a lot of people fall into quite a normal and logical trap. I call it a trap; others may call it appropriate exposition. The lights come up to expose a group of four or five players, and someone makes the move to "corral" the group with an all-encompassing expositional lasso:

> *Okay, you guys. Welcome to the first day of class. Everybody find a seat. We are about to begin!*

Or:

Okay, line up everybody! This is the army! I'm your drill
sergeant, not your mother. Line up!

Remember, I called it a trap and others might call it an
appropriate expositional tool or a good move. I don't mind the
expositional element as much as the fear and accessories that come
with it. The fear part is the tinge of panic at the top. It's the kind of
"Okay, everybody" or "Okay, guys" that your teacher would throw
at you in fifth grade to gain control out of disorder. It certainly
comes out of a slight need to corral the scene in that way. It also
comes with the feeling of starting at the very beginning as opposed
to starting in the middle. In the above examples, the "welcome,"
the "first day of class," and the "this is the army" are all things we
might say at the beginning of something. This happens frequently
in long form by responsible, good improvisers. They want to create
order out of potential chaos.

Quite often, when five people come out of the back line or
the lights come up to reveal five people, there *is* chaos. There are
a couple of people doing little more than standing, there may be
one person doing business by themselves in the environment, and
perhaps there is one person doing something very kinetic, all of
which may or may not have one or more people saying something
out loud. The first impulse is to contain this disparate energy and
create order. So we say things like, "Welcome to camp, everyone!
Find your buddy for the buddy system." Introductory exposition
to corral the group. I would like for us to look at this for a bit
both so that you can recognize these moves in your ensemble, and
so that you may finesse them with greater complexity and explore
substantive alternatives, as well.

This exercise comes in three parts.

EXPOSITION EXERCISE, PART ONE

Have your group do a bunch of group scenes, one after another, that absolutely *do* use these exposition devices at the beginning. Your goal is to initiate as many as you can. I want you and your group to identify the attributes of these overly obvious expositional moves. I'll help you with these common examples:

> *Welcome to...*
> *Thank you for coming, everybody. Let's get started...*
> *Okay, you guys. Let's begin...*
> *You may wonder why I called you here...*
> *All right everybody. Gather round...*

As you do a bunch of these, have someone in the ensemble, whether in the scene or not (or the director), call "scene" each time. There is no need to let these scenes go on for long, just long enough to notice the quality of the content of the scene after executing one of these expositional lines.

The purpose of the first part of this is to have fun identifying the characteristics of that kind of contrived expositional line and to check out what kind of dialogue ensues. The scene that follows that type of expositional device is almost always one where the characters don't know each other and share no familiar past. It is often a tentative, authority-driven (teacher, drill sergeant, camp counselor, etc.) scene where people don't know, or maybe know but don't really like, other characters in the scene. All of this is quite okay for an improv scene, don't get me wrong. You could very well have a fun and powerful scene out of a choice about a classroom on the first day of school among people who don't know or like each other, and kill it. As I write this, I am reviewing in my mind the classroom scenes that I have put onstage myself, in narrative or sketch comedy shows, that worked great. The problem is the space of fear and control that many of these moves come from in long form, and the limiting "beginning" parameters that it forces the group scenes into time after time after time.

Do this exercise for a half hour, and you will begin to realize the quality of such an initiation. As you get past my examples above and find derivations, notice that nearly all of the moves control and corral the group, and that many of them start at the beginning, not in the middle, of something.

EXPOSITION EXERCISE, PART TWO

Now do a bunch of scenes that do *not* start with a corralling exposition. Make a choice to eliminate anything that sounds like the above examples. Do a bunch of scenes for nine minutes, and then stop and discuss the attributes of these types of beginnings and what they do for the resulting scene. It may be hard to manufacture actual words making this shift between these two experiences, but grind through it and let it burn a little until you find the zone.

EXPOSITION EXERCISE, PART THREE

Do part one of this exercise again, but this time start in the middle of a sentence.

So instead of:

> *Okay, class, settle down. As you know, we have a pop quiz today, everybody take a seat.*

It would start:

> *...number three on our pop quiz, "Who was our president during the War of 1812?"*

The second initiation is what a teacher would say if the lights came up and you were in the middle of a classroom scene. There would be no need for a label of where they are or what they were doing, and there would be an assumption of a shared past among the people in the scene.

Another example pair:

> *Welcome to book club, everybody. Let's take a seat...*
>
> vs.
>
> *...and this is why Ayn Rand had Howard Roark laugh in the very first line of* The Fountainhead.

The second initiation is what you might hear if you happened upon the middle of a book club scene. You may be thinking, "But how would the other players know exactly where they are? How would everyone know what the initiating person meant?" It is true that in the second example, no book club is mentioned. It could be a college professor finishing a lecture. It could be friends at lunch or book reviewers. It could be anything!

Exactly. Who gives a damn? A savvy ensemble of improvisers wouldn't care. They would be excited about an initiation open to numerous possibilities. A savvy group would be delighted that the premise and circumstances aren't so obvious. The collective discovery based on acceptance would be fun for both the players and the audience, and it cuts out a lot of unsophisticated expository bullshit at the beginning of the scene. Long form is long, but the real estate of time is still quite valuable.

People who make corralling expositions in long form are attempting to control an idea and the people of the scene, and while it's a rather noble gesture to bring order to what may seem like chaos, it often comes off as a bit fake and contrived. In contrast, the group that starts a little bit more subtly in the middle of the scene shows a more layered, deft approach to their work. This gives the group greater confidence, trust, and a healthy dose of "fuck it" mentality.

Practicing these more nuanced initiations could eventually help your ensemble become more aware of these types of expositional moves in order to build a solid scene from them. If, after this exercise, you and your group are having trouble getting on the same page, this next exercise may help. It is about quickly acknowledging a suggestion in a group scene or game.

ACKNOWLEDGMENT EXERCISE

Do a series of short group scenes where each player will end up having only one or two lines of dialogue in the scene. The goal is for everyone to acknowledge the first person's suggestion, no matter what it is.

For this exercise, I want you to think of the word "acknowledge" in a literal way. Listen to an initiation by the first person in the scene, lift an operative word or concept from their initiation, and use it in your response. I want you to borrow a word or concept in this exercise because I want your acknowledgment to be overly obvious. The initiation can be anything, but the initiator gets bonus points for a sentence that starts in the middle of something.

Let me provide a couple of examples of how this exercise should proceed. It's a bit tricky, and as they say in learning card magic, it takes a little knack. A little practice.

IMPROVISER A: *(Initiates.)* The sky is so blue.

IMPROVISER B: The sky is very blue in Montana.

IMPROVISER C: A blue sky cheers me up.

I feel like a second grader with this simplistic example, but it demonstrates that what matters is the very basic idea of lifting a word from the initiation and using it in the response.

Another example:

IMPROVISER A: *(Initiates.)* I'm getting out of this warehouse!

IMPROVISER B: You are staying in this warehouse, you son of a bitch.

IMPROVISER C: The cops have got this place surrounded.

This lifts the word "warehouse," acknowledges it, and then builds from there.

Looks like "yes, and…"

Yes, and yet it doesn't have to be.

IMPROVISER A: *(Initiates.)* I'm getting out of this warehouse!

IMPROVISER B: There's no getting out.

IMPROVISER C: Is this a warehouse? It looks like a candy factory to me.

IMPROVISER D: Whatever it is, we are leaving now!

This example has questions and even a denial of the location. It doesn't matter for this exercise as long as the initiation is acknowledged.

So, practice acknowledging for a bit. The tendency is for this exercise to be very thinky. Let it be in the beginning. It can often feel like a chess match.

IMPROVISER A: *(Initiates.)* The sky is so blue.

IMPROVISER B: *(Three-second beat.)* Yes. Montana has lots of blue sky.

IMPROVISER C: *(Four-second pause.)* A blue sky often means a happy day ahead.

IMPROVISER D: *(Three-second beat.)* The clouds are pretty against the blue.

If it is this slow and tedious in the beginning, let it be. After a bit, though, *speed it up!* Try combining it with the two-line scene exercise from the chapter on editing. Have this exercise evolve to the point where there are no pauses at all between the dialogue. It needs to go lightning fast. Do it both ways: very slow and thought-filled, and then very fast with no pauses at all.

What will you notice? Both have value, but I bet your ensemble can get to the same space in a group scene much faster than you thought. Try it in many different ways with many different types of lines and many different styles and degrees of stakes in the initiations. You may be amazed at how quickly you and your group learn to assimilate to the acknowledged space in the group scenes. Make a game out of how fast your group can acknowledge the initiation and develop it into set circumstances in the scene. Now imagine that in performance.

Also practice going from very obvious initiations, like "the sky is so blue," to more vague conceptual initiations, like "Dreary was his middle name," and see what your group is able to latch on to. You will soon see that the initiation itself *doesn't matter* as long as something is grabbed and the pattern of acknowledgment is declared and executed.

Now, let's add characters…

CHARACTER EXERCISE

Do a series of scenes with each actor portraying a vastly different character than the other actors, all while acknowledging the initiated content. Challenge yourselves to create disparate character energies while maintaining the same focus on acknowledging the actual content by lifting words.

You will notice that although the characters are very different, the content acknowledgment brings the scene together in the minds of both actors and audience members. It could be a Russian guy, a homeless woman, a queen, and a wood sprite all speaking about the Moors of Scotland. The shared, acknowledged content keeps the scene aligned.

Now, close your eyes. (But actually don't because then you wouldn't be able to continue reading this.)

MOVEMENT EXERCISE

Have five people position themselves onstage and close their eyes. Each person, with eyes closed, gets into a physical activity or an individual character space of movement. After a bit, either the director or another player calls "scene." The players open their eyes and continue their physical business. They then perform the acknowledgment exercises while maintaining the physical movements and characters they've created. One player initiates, and the others immediately acknowledge. Their physical associations help them form distinct character voices as they execute lines of dialogue that very quickly acknowledge the initiation.

Do this entire exercise seventeen times with your ensemble, keeping the scenes short with only a couple of lines per player. You will learn that you can surprise yourself and others and still acknowledge the content together no matter how different the characters are to begin with.

The setup for this exercise comes close to the real-life scenario that often happens in long form where the lights come up to find you and your cast doing five completely different things. It's a mess.

Practicing disparate energies or characters as a group and simply acknowledging something over and over will make your ensemble much more proactive and productive in group scenes, no matter how strange the scene seems at first. Your ensemble won't *freak out* as much and instead will become *conditioned* to keeping a clear, collective head when managing these group scenes and games. As with anything in improvisation, this practice doesn't ensure a hundred-percent success, but it drastically improves your ability to function in group scenes. Acknowledging content in this way gives your brain a healthier thing to think about than what it usually is thinking about in group scenes:

1. What the hell is everyone doing?

2. Why the hell are they doing that?

3. I don't know what to do or say, so I'll keep dancing like an idiot.

If a group can come to a consensus and practice this, then group scenes and games will not throw them and instead will invite an active, positive choice. This is a good first step to a great group scene.

If you can do the above exercise, then this next one will be a breeze. It's one of my favorites. At first, it appears to be a character exercise, but it is actually most helpful in regard to group scenes.

SAME CHARACTER EXERCISE

Form a back line. At any point, someone can step forward and start a monologue while traveling a couple steps downstage, making it a strong choice with a fairly big vocal and physical initiation. After watching for a couple of seconds, the remaining players in the back line also step forward and take on the exact same character created by the initiator with the exact same physical characteristics and voice. Each player maintains the presentational monologue and does not address any other person onstage. After each person settles solidly into the character, stop, get back in line, and repeat. Do this eleven or twelve times.

Now, do the same thing but eliminate the "watching" part. Yes. *Immediately* do the initiated character. Do it absolutely immediately in point-two seconds. Every individual in every group can *immediately* get the energy of another individual and immediately *become* the interpretation of their exact character. Do this fourteen times.

You can begin to see why this is both a good character and a good group exercise.

But we're not done yet. Now take this to a scenic level. Instead of talking all at once in monologue, a player steps out of the line and begins a scene as a character. Again, for the purposes of this exercise, I invite strong and big vocal and physical choices. Another improviser, without any time going by, responds in the scene as the initiator's exact same character. Then a third actor joins, again as the same character. Then a fourth. Now there are four people onstage who have acknowledged the *character* initiation so much that they have actually taken on the exact same character.

Does the audience feel like the other actors have cheated or stolen the first actor's character? Hell, no. They are just thinking, "Oh, four British guys," or, "Look, a group of wood sprites." For the audience, it is an immediate acceptance of the space that has been created for them, and they are ready to just sit back and enjoy the scene. Does the initiator feel ripped off by the other players copying her character? No, she does not. What she does feel is affirmation that what she created was accepted and acknowledged so much that her fellow improvisers have taken the same character for themselves. "Now we are in the same space" is what everyone is thinking, including the audience.

This tool works well in three-person scenes, entering scenes, and even two-person scenes. Taking on your scene partner's energy every once in a while is rarely a bad idea. In the arena of personal growth, it will take you to places you've never been before with your improvisation. It may not occur to you to be a wood sprite or a groggy astronaut on your own, but when your partner creates it and you take it on, you will travel to new places.

CHARACTER OF THE SPACE EXERCISE

There is one last exercise I want to throw at you. It comes to me via Martin de Maat via Josephine Forsberg via Viola Spolin herself. I know it by the name Character of the Space. I think this exercise happens to embody everything wonderful about improvisation, and I will tell you why after I guide you through it. It is a sound and movement transformation exercise that you have probably already rehearsed and performed in some manner or another. In various derivations, it is performed as a game or as an opener in long form everywhere. This is my approach, and I am going to go through it as if an ensemble of improvisers is in the room and I am guiding this exercise the way it was taught to me.

> *I want you to walk around the room. Just walk around the room in silence. Just walk around at random in silence.*

> *Good.*

Now, start casually looking at each other. You may laugh or smile or whatever, that's fine. Just continue walking and look at each other as you pass by.

Yes.

Now I'd like you to notice the speed at which everyone is walking, and I want you all to walk at the same pace, the same speed.

Now continue looking at each other, and I want to challenge you all to have the same expression, the same look, more or less, on your faces.

If there is an emotion attached to that, become that emotion. So everyone is the same... same pace and same emotion. Now look at arms and hands. Make sure that they are the same as well. Same pace, same look, and same arms...

Good.

Now, when I say "go," someone make a very subtle move with your head, arms, or hands. When that person makes that slight move, everyone immediately, but subtly, take on that movement and continue doing it over and over, all together.

Go.

Great.

Keep doing that, and now put just a little energy into that move and let it, if it wants to, transform into another move. Slowly... so no one person is changing it up. Have it be that it changes organically. No need to force it.

Good. Keep moving all the same—all the same pace and actions and expression.

Now when I say "go," someone make a subtle sound. Make a little sound and put it out there.

Ready... a subtle sound... and go.

Good. Now, everyone take on that sound and repeat it, keeping the physical in the same place with everyone else and adding the sound. Keep the physical the same and the sound. Now add energy to the sound, whatever that means to all of you, very slowly so that no one person sticks out. Just add a bit more energy to the sound and movement and allow it to transform all together. Have it be important to you that everyone is keeping the same sounds and movement and that we are adding energy and allowing it to transform.

Good.

At this point, I usually just shut up. There is now a group of people doing a collective dance with sound and movement. It goes up and down in volume, and the movement keeps transforming and changing subtly. The physical score of the group changes organically. Every once in a while, you might catch someone making a move that sticks out a little, and when they do, everyone else immediately adapts to it and maintains and transforms that movement along with the sound. Seriously, at this point I could just walk out of the room. I could easily let this go on for a half an hour, and I have many times in the past.

It is quite lovely.

I always remember the first time I do something. First times are meaningful, and I want to remember. The first time I did Character of the Space, I remember being in a real "zone" with my fellow improvisers. Yes, it felt a little "80s Actor Exercise" and probably had some *Godspell* and *Pippin* influence, but it was, nonetheless, a great experience.

I mentioned that I think this exercise *embodies* improvisation. I do. I feel it is a great model for improvisation because it forms a group of people who are choosing to work together to create an amazing space of ever-changing initiation, acceptance, heightening, surprise, and transformation. Every initiation made by anyone at all is immediately accepted and adapted with absolutely no judgment by anyone else in the group. It is not only immediately accepted, but once it is collectively executed, it is heightened. This commitment to what has been created offers turns and surprises not only to those watching, but also to the players within. The acceptance and heightening allows for transformation within the piece.

It truly looks choreographed.

Initiation, acceptance, heightening, surprise, and transformation are words I may use to describe a great improv scene or a great long form itself. As I said, Character of the Space embodies that.

I have seen this done so well at the beginning of a long form that it is mesmerizing, and I have seen it completely butchered. It is an indicator of an ensemble and their collective thinking, for sure. When it works, it is a beautiful dance, launched by the suggestion and explored in a lovely, surprising, and very funny way. But it doesn't work when there is judgment, contrived initiations, or transformations pushing too much toward one person's agenda, or when there are choices made that are obviously opposite of that which is happening in the moment.

The ones that don't work always end up with the group looking at each other and digging, moving their hands as if they are in the wind, and/or saying "whoosh" over and over. I am only half-kidding, as this example is widely known to many as a model for a bad long form opener.

At any rate, Character of the Space is a beautiful thing. As you probably know by now, I am not big on warm-ups, but if you have the space and time before a show, this is a great warm-up.

Character of the Space also embodies every other exercise I have offered in this chapter leading up to it. Every single one of them is about immediately identifying and accepting an energy, then acting without judgment based on that initiation. All of these exercises, and the thinking behind them, aren't really that new. For me, it is just a way of illustrating what great long form groups already do in a group scenario:

1. They initiate quickly and start in the middle.

2. They have absolutely no judgment about each other's initiations.

3. They quickly affirm each other, accepting, executing, and adding to the initiation.

4. They surprise and allow the scene, game, or the show itself to transform.

Whether by choice, their experience together, or both, great improv groups can finish each other's thoughts. It looks like they know each other's moves. They are confident and not freaking out. They are funny. They are not saying a bunch of bullshit.

That's what ensembles who choose this type of powerful acceptance in their work manage to do and what improvisation calls the "group mind." To me, it is not something magical or ethereal. It is simply collective choice, courage, and integrity to accept what is happening and uphold the agreed-upon vision of the ensemble in general.

Any opener, group scene, game, or closer in long form can benefit greatly from rehearsing the exercises in this chapter. I challenge you to challenge yourselves with this vital and exciting way of looking at group work. Your group can absolutely achieve a powerful, intelligent, funny, and entertaining group mind.

You can do it this afternoon.

14

SAME NOT DIFFERENT

I WANT TO discuss a few seemingly unrelated moves in improv that, believe it or not, have a lot in common. While I've mentioned some of them previously, let's fully define each and discuss how they function in long form.

Callback

A callback is when an operative of a scene, like a theme, line, reference, or action, is extracted and brought back in another scene, usually for a laugh. Whatever is brought or called back will hopefully be recognized from earlier so it can either be referenced in a slightly different context or brought out full-on as an extension of the previous, usually funny, idea.

Runner

A runner occurs when the exact same construct used in one scene is extended later in its own beat or slot in the running order. A runner revisits the same scene, characters, or idea throughout the show at different times. Runners are usually short scenes, but long enough to establish the same comedic construct. A callback has more impact and punch than a runner, which re-visits an idea more fully.

Tag Out

A tag out is essentially a condensed runner. A player from the back line "tags out" another player in a scene and takes their place as a different character. The player or players that are not tagged out remain the same. Tag outs take an idea or operative content and immediately call it back, over and over, in a succession of improvised beats.

Time Jump

A time jump in long form is a device that allows the audience to recognize that, although we are visiting the same characters, location, or premise of an earlier scene, the timing is different, either leaping forward or sometimes reverting to the past. Of course, time jumps are a necessary and age-old narrative convention, but the time jump has become long form improv's own signature convention for forwarding scenes within the form.

Walk Through

A walk through occurs when someone walks through a scene, riding over or through an operative feature of the scene and hopefully getting a laugh without too much disruption.

Entrance

An entrance is when someone enters in the middle of a scene. Walk-ons and entrances can enhance or sink a scene, depending on how they are approached.

I know you may already have an understanding of these improv moves, but let's use some examples to see how they function in long form.

> **SCENE**: *A father and son. The father wants the kid to do chores. The kid is agreeable, but each time the father suggests doing something like mowing the lawn or cleaning a room, the kid says he will after the watching the show. Halfway through the scene...*
>
> **FATHER**: If you don't get off your ass and mow the grass right now, I am going to beat you and ground you for a week.
>
> **KID**: Sure. Makes perfect sense, Dad. Just need to find out how this *Lockup* episode ends.

Not hilarious, but you get the point, or at least you understand the respective points of view. Let's look at some of the moves as applied to the scene above, and see what they have in common. I'll start with a simple entrance.

I'm going to enter the scene, and I'm going to enter as the mother. The first instinct people usually have when entering a scene is to "think different" or objectify the scene. My suggestion is that the first step to entering a scene could be to think *same*, not different. In this scene, the first instinct would be for the mother to walk into the conflict between the father and son and seek to resolve it, to objectify the scene by asking why they are fighting, or to suggest that they "fight too often" or that they "always fight in the living room," etc. This would be the normal choice—to speak "at" the conflict and justify it somehow. Not the funny or interesting choice, but the normal choice.

The more interesting choice, ironically, is the *same* choice, not the different one. In this case, having the mother make the same choice as something that is already happening in the scene, such as another character's point of view or emotional state, would be refreshing to the audience.

> **FATHER:** If you don't get off your ass and mow the grass right now, I am going to beat you and ground you for a week.

> **KID:** Sure. Makes perfect sense, Dad. Just need to find out how this *Lockup* episode ends. *(MOTHER ENTERS in a rush.)*

> **FATHER:** Can't you do anything about this, honey?

> **MOTHER:** I will, just as soon as this episode of *Sister Wives* ends in the other room.

> Or...

> **MOTHER:** *(ENTERS.)* Tommy, if you don't mow the lawn right now—right now—we are going to send you to a summer camp you will not survive!

The audience will appreciate seeing a *different* choice than what they expected with an entrance, and this subversion of expectation is often taking the *same* point of view of something that exists in the scene already. Resolving the conflict is a predictable choice. Heightening the conflict by taking on an existing point of view is surprising and funny.

In all of the confusion of long form improvisation, the audience needs to be able to grasp onto patterns as much as possible. Thinking the same in an entrance is a catalyst for propelling a scene. In a television crime drama, imagine a small town sheriff's department working on a crime when the FBI gets involved.

Wouldn't it be refreshing if the sheriff was actually just fine with the FBI being there, and the FBI didn't pander or think they knew the "real way of doing things" and had to "school the country folk?" It's kind of like that.

Sameness is actually the common element among all of the improvisational and long form moves and techniques listed above. It's the reason I grouped them together, actually. In all of these, it is vital to hone in on the commonalities of the scene in order to successfully execute the move. "What is the dominant energy that I can capture and then use?" Yes, it is boring when you break it down, but it is beneficial to realize what makes these techniques work. If a player is thinking about sameness and pattern, then he is a step ahead of the person who is thinking about resolving conflict or objectifying the scene.

Let's look at another move: the callback. If I wanted to call back something later on in the show from an earlier scene, I would have to consider a couple of things:

1. Is there something, like a word, phrase, reaction, character choice, physical action, etc., that "rang out" enough in that scene that the audience would recognize it if I reference it later? (I used the term "rang out" on purpose, because I often think of notable content, such as physical initiations or operative words, as if one is "ringing a bell" in the scene. Every time performers ring it later, it calls it back for the audience.)

2. How can I convey the quality of sameness and at the same time start in the middle with my scene or callback?

In the father/son example, were there enough times that the son, and then the mom, deflected chores or responsibility by needing to finish a TV show that the idea could be called back later in the show? In an unrelated scene ten minutes later, a boss asks an employee to finish a report, only to have the employee say, "Absolutely, as soon as I finish watching *Hoarders* on my iPad." If I was to get really technical, does the callback deal specifically with reality TV? Is that reality TV slant (*Lockup, Sister Wives, Hoarders*) part of the playable energy in the scene that will call back? The art of the callback definitely has a subjective learning curve, including having you first dismiss the idea of doing something different, and instead embrace the idea of identifying a pattern that rings out in the scene. *That* is the thing that will call back effectively.

A runner, which is a series of callbacks, relies on that sameness as well. With a runner in our example, the bell would be rung so much that by the time it was called back two or three times in the show, almost anything could be said with the response, "Yes, as soon as I finish watching…" After numerous repetitions, it could even develop out of its initial limitations while still maintaining the sameness necessary for the bell ring. For example, the response could become, "Yes, as soon as I finish listening to this podcast," or "Yes, as soon as I finish this game of Candy Crush," thus moving away from the limitation to reality TV shows. Sure, this is getting a bit mathematical, but it is rooted in identifying operative dominant energy based on a recognizable pattern.

Let's look at tag outs. In a tag out, the sameness has to be identified very quickly. What is the immediate dominant energy in the scene? In the father/son example, how can I tag this out?

FATHER: If you don't get off your ass and mow the grass right now, I am going to beat you and ground you for a week.

KID: Sure. Makes perfect sense, Dad. Just need to find out how this *Lockup* episode ends.

I have to get the sameness of one of the points of view, not the difference, for the tag out to work properly. So let's say another improviser tags out the guy playing the father and becomes a police officer.

> **OFFICER**: Son, I have pulled you over because you were speeding. May I see your license?
>
> **KID**: Yeah, just let me finish listening to this Foo Fighters song.

In this tag out, he wasn't really able to call back anything of value for the audience to latch on to. There simply isn't a bell to ring in the officer's line. But what if the player tags out the kid and becomes a doctor?

> **DOCTOR**: Just hang in there, Gary. I'll finish your colonoscopy as soon as I'm done watching this YouTube video.

In these examples, the "guy who avoids doing something until he finishes with entertainment" has more recognizable energy than the "guy wanting the other guy to do something." For a tag out, it is important to be able to identify the dominant energy of a scene quickly in order to reproduce it effectively.

Time jump. Same thing. Often the location, characters, or circumstance will carry enough sameness to launch the next scene after a time jump. Build off the one that has the impact necessary to create the strongest recall for the audience.

Let's say you are doing a scene where you are locked in a walk-in freezer. The scene is absolutely based on the fact that you cannot get out. Now, it may be that this circumstance isn't really what's driving the scene, but it will definitely have great recall value for the audience. For example, perhaps while you are locked in the freezer, your scene partner reveals that he is a Christian, and the scene is actually about deflecting Christian preaching *while* being trapped in a walk-in freezer. While the preaching is what drives the scene, the second those same actors are back in the freezer later on in the show, there would be instant recall for the audience. That location and circumstance would have the greater dominant energy and thus would be the quickest way to get back to that scene. One pound on the wall and one scream, and we have jumped back to being locked in the freezer. The players now have the freedom and the ability to continue that scene at any point in time they wish.

While being locked in the freezer is a very strong choice for a successful time jump for this scene, it is not the only option. The actor playing the Christian character could use preaching as a content pattern to recall, and it would probably recall fairly quickly. Of course, in a situation like this, the savvy choice for the other actor would be to have them now stuck in an elevator or something instead of a freezer. The audience would then clearly get that this is a different point in time and that the characters are stuck together again. "Stuck" and "preaching" work together as the operatives in this time jump. These are both elements that have enough dominant energy to successfully recall, yet still allow more flexibility to the remaining choices of time and place.

The key to a successful time jump is to choose the elements with the greater dominant energy. Let's say you and your scene partner are two Irish guys with thick dialects, shoeing horses in a barn. Four scenes go by in the show, and you'd like to call back these characters. "Barn" or "shoeing horses" isn't the dominant playable energy in this scene since "Irish" and "Irish dialect" would definitely have faster recall with the audience. The new scene could have them in a bowling alley. It doesn't matter, as long as they are Irish.

Let's look at one last example. A scene has three people weeping because they lost their jobs. They are crying loudly in a restaurant. In this case, "crying" just might be the playable energy to call back for a time jump forward. It could be in a car or a bar, who cares? The second these three start crying about anything, the *emotion* will be recognizable to the audience.

EXERCISE

I invite you to do this exercise not only for the "same" moves discussed in this chapter, but also to practice identifying the dominant energy in group scenes and in improvisation in general. It is one of the most fun and most valuable life exercises I can think of to learn to ask, "What is this situation *about*? What is the dominant energy? What is really going on?"

The exercise is merely observation, but in a particular way. I want you to observe human interactions around you and hone in and identify the quality or qualities that you would latch on to in order to call back, tag out, jump forward, or enter that scene. What is the dominant energy, that operative behavior, content, emotion, or character attribute that rings "loudest" in the human experience you are observing?

Let's say you are at a coffee shop and there are two high school girls sitting at a table next to you. These girls are talking about guys at their school. Is it the actual content of "talking about guys" that you would enter, start doing, and join in on if that were a scene? Is that what would let you "glide into" this scene with the most ease? To call it back or jump it forward? Perhaps the girls are saying the word "like" a million times. Would that be it? Or both? Perhaps one girl is playing with her hair, and the other is playing with a ring. "Playing with objects and fidgeting" may be the operative moves to bring to light in a callback. Maybe.

Now you are sitting on a bus, and there's a guy sitting across from you listening to music. What is the operative energy here? Is he singing along? Is he looking out the window? What characteristic could you latch on to if you wanted to "call him back"? It may be a very subtle observation, but that is the point. Look for every opportunity to grab something based in sameness and pattern. Practice identifying these qualities, from emotion to language to character traits to style to voice to points of view, and you will not only be practicing these for the conventions of this chapter, but for what's going on in improvisation more broadly. This skill is the essence of getting what a scene is about and learning what to gravitate toward while you are improvising entrances, time cuts, or often the scene as a whole.

> *What is it about that guy? Does he elongate his end-vowels? What's going on with those kids? That one kid is obsessed with trucks. He has a truck-thing. Why does my mom always try to make everything about her? That is a consistent behavior pattern. What is it about that girl? What is the thing about these two? What is it?*

Same.

15

STRAY CATS

TWO-PERSON LONG FORM

Two-person long form is a wonderful thing in the world of improvisation: two people improvising together for a half hour, forty-five minutes, or an hour, using a single suggestion. I have had the pleasure of doing two-person shows countless times with some of the best improvisers in the United States, including Jimmy Carrane, Stephnie Weir, Robert Dassie, Susan Messing, T. J. Jagodowski, Scott Adsit, and David Pasquesi. I don't want to write extensively about two-person long form because I know that as I write this, David Pasquesi and T. J. Jagodowski have just published their book, *Improvisation at the Speed of Life*, and Susan Messing is writing one. I will leave it to their insight and expertise, for they are truly the best. Susan is an all-star at two-person long form with unrelated scenes inspired by a single suggestion, and T. J. and Dave are experts at improvising a single piece based on a single suggestion.

All I really want to say about it is… do it. It is scary, so do it. This evening. Find a person with whom you like improvising, get in a room for an hour, and improvise. It is an exhilarating, whirl-wind experience that will amaze and surprise you. As improvisers, we often think that we don't have any more to give when we are improvising, or that we can't hold on to a character or point of view for all that long. Two-person improv cures you of that fear and disability and provides an ironically safe place to explore when you think you wouldn't have anything else to offer. You always have more and can always find another angle in which to explore a game, a character, or a point of view. It is delirious, and you truly do get swept up into an intuitive, intellectual brain-collision of pure rush and fun. These are the shows that we don't remem-ber, for we are too busy playing around and immersing ourselves in fun.

Try it.

The other thing I might offer is to jump in without the burden of gaining your audience's laughter. That's a stiff way of saying, "Don't go for laughs." Play it straight up, without feeling like you are joking the scene away. Just like I discussed earlier, it is okay, even great, to aim for laughs, but forcing jokes will only interfere with your ability to let go, play, and have fun.

There is a different way of being funny in improv: be organic to the scene, slower, and more substantive. The laugh, when it comes, is richer, for it truly comes from the audience's and the performers' newfound, learned, collective, familiar past of circumstance and character background. That means that both the improvisers and the audience are patient. We can absorb and immerse ourselves in the reality of the improvised relationship and the depth of prem-ise. The integrity of each moment, without the need to fill a laugh quota, builds one upon the other. When the laugh comes, it is a different *kind* of improv laugh. It is a laugh that is born of more empathetic and substantive truth, based on each previous moment built by the characters' relationship.

This is where improvisation defies my cynical saying, "Improvisation: always different, always the same," for it is a different construct of improvisational outcomes. Unpredictable and real.

I'll stop now, and let those who do two-person long form so very well explore their processes in their own books.

But do give it a shot, won't you?

PRE-SHOW WARM-UPS

I go back and forth between whether I find a warm-up before a show valuable or not. It sure as hell seems like it would be valuable. What possibly could be the harm of a warm-up before a show? Well… maybe there isn't any harm, and maybe there is. And maybe it's just me. But I go back to my own equation about improvisation when I challenge the idea of warming up before a show.

The more importance you place on an improv experience, the less likely you are to play.

Going into a show, whatever makes it "important" in my mind are the things that are going to start me thinking too much in a bad way. Many times, a warm-up does just that for me. It adds gravity to the improv show that I'm getting ready to do. It makes me feel like the experience is so important that we have to go through some *ritual* of preparation beforehand, which in and of itself gets me thinking in a less carefree way. It stresses the perception that I should be treating this with a lot more reverence, even though it's still just making up words in a comedy show.

Then, there's the actual choice of the warm-up itself. Zip Zap Zop just doesn't do it for me, and after a couple of decades, throwing an imaginary ball around a circle just doesn't get the ol' brain firing, either.

I was the guy who always did the warm-up because I thought I should and because of "support your partner" and those other positive ensemble ideals. The truth is that I often felt really stupid and uncommitted. For me, the warm-up was confirming that I felt anti-playful as evidenced by the exercise itself, and now I was carrying *that* feeling into the long form I was getting ready to improvise. And that feeling did indeed carry. I could never give myself over to the warm-up completely, and like I said, the very idea or execution of the warm-up itself raised the idea of "importance" in my mind. Blah.

Now the flip side: a bunch of half-drunk idiots who are going onstage with you and not taking anything seriously in a very destructive, self-sabotaging way need to get their shit together, center their focus, and ground themselves. In situations like this, warming up raises the importance of the show in a good way. It brings everyone together on the same page and aligns the agreement that we are all endeavoring to create this thing together, and we're going to support each other out there.

I go back and forth. I think my only advice, really, is to know all of this and take from the warm-up what *you* want. Don't beat yourself up if this warm-up seems stupid or that warm-up makes you feel like you can't "let go." Everyone has varying degrees of commitment and freedom with different warm-up experiences, and it doesn't have to greatly influence the improv show you are about to do. Take it with a grain of salt.

While keeping three different colors of imaginary balls in the air might help some people discover point of view, relationship, what the scene is about, and playful content in their improvisation, it never did that much for me. That said, I have done 7,453 warm-ups, so who am I to say? This quantity of warm-ups actually might be the reason I'm such a bitch about it. Perhaps the rage I held each time I was zapping and zopping was the driving hateful force behind my power as an improviser. Could be.

MONOLOGUES IN LONG FORM

Whether it be a character monologue or one coming straight from you and your experiences, start in the middle, start in the middle, and start in the middle of the monologue. Gosh, nothing is so un-dramatic, non-attention getting, and basically boring as a monologue starting with the amazing words "When I was in college, I…" or "When I was twenty-five and…" or "Last year, when I…"

These are just as bad, exposition-laden, and anti-theatrical as a stand-up comedian delivering "Have you ever noticed…" and "Has this ever happened to you?" when launching their material. Start in the middle.

And I never saw Billy again.

Now spend the body of the monologue leading back up to that statement. Come around, and by the end, we should know why you never saw Billy again.

You don't always have to come back around, though, to have a strong monologue that starts in the middle.

That's when I knew I didn't have a shot.

We in the audience do not know exactly what the improviser is talking about at this point, and that's a *good* thing. Is the story about not having a line of sight for a gun? Is it about not having enough whiskey to drink a shot? Is it about basketball? Is it about not having a vaccine?

> *I was behind the eight ball good, but I lined up my cue anyway.*

Ah, it's about pool, and we are in the *middle* of the game.

Now, whether performed as a character monologue or as oneself, this is a powerful tool. Starting in the middle of a monologue does the same thing that starting in the middle of an improv scene does:

1. It puts you in the midst of something, of a continuum.

2. It already has spontaneous stakes attached.

3. It assumes a familiar past with relationships and circumstances.

With a monologue, this approach also does two more things: it usually tips off the audience to expect a monologue as opposed to a line of dialogue, and it grabs more focus than if you were to begin with a line of exposition.

EXERCISE

Practice going into a monologue by starting a sentence in the middle. With each new monologue, switch characters or toggle between a character and yourself each time. Keep each mini-monologue to just a few sentences, and make sure that each initiation starts in the middle of the story.

At first, literally say the word "and" at the beginning of each first sentence of each monologue.

> *...and that's how the shovel got into the car.*

> *...and that's why it's not working out for you here at the warehouse.*

Then do the same thing, but don't use the word "and." Huh? Simply remove the word "and," but continue to start in the middle.

That's how the shovel got into the car.

That's why it's not working out for you here at the warehouse.

This puts you in the middle without having to literally use the word "and" every time.

Do this nineteen times, with nineteen different monologues starting in the middle and each only a few sentences long. This is a really challenging but fun way (and I pretty much hate the word "fun") to put the first line out there with conviction and then let your brain and mouth catch up to it.

If you are courageous enough to practice just going for your first line with commitment, then you are simultaneously training yourself to initiate more freely and to gain the skill of confidently catching up with your initiation no matter what it is. One of the great things about this exercise is that it is very difficult to backtrack in the assumption of information. Using one of my examples above, if you say, "That's why it's not working out for you here at the warehouse," it's not really possible to go backwards to create a bullshit introductory exposition. The sentence assumes that your character knows someone else who works at a warehouse, and that the past circumstances of the job have led up to this point in the conversation. You're simply not going to say, "That's why it's not working out for you here at the warehouse," as your first sentence, and then have your next sentence be, "Yeah, here I am… in this warehouse…"

Now I'm going to flip a bit. If you practice this enough with your improvised monologues, you can *then* give yourself the permission to actually choose to go back and start a monologue with the kind of beginning exposition I scorned earlier. For example, practice one out of every five initiations with the type of expository line I asked you to remove, like, "When I was a kid, my father… "

If you practice initiating in the middle of your circumstance often, you will then notice that when you *do* start with "beginning-type" exposition, your introductions will now have much more power attached to them. The beginning won't be as weak, or look like you are searching for something, or as vague as before. Instead, because you practiced the idea of starting with conviction in an already assumed point of view or emotional state, your exposition-laden monologue initiations are likely to have higher stakes, stronger reactions, and a more focused point of view. They will be as vital, theatrical, confident, and invested as the ones that start in the middle. All of this is the result of practicing making dynamic choices.

One additional note about monologues: when you do a monologue that is from or about the actual "you," be honest. Do not lie or we will know it, and you will look like an asshole liar.

NOTES AFTER THE SHOW

What does your ensemble do after a long form show? Do you sit, have a beer, and lightly talk about the show, both the good and the bad, the fun and the laughs, barely remembering and then talking about whatever with another beer?

Or do you sit for an hour and go through every single moment of every single scene and every single game step-by-step-by-step, tearing it apart and beating yourselves up, dissecting, talking, and analyzing for at least an hour and fifteen long minutes sucked into the excruciating abyss of meaningless anger-filled frustrating intellectualization, suffering moment by moment, ripping and shredding and clawing what little residue of fun is left out of an otherwise perfectly lovely evening?

Which do you do?

Don't forget.

It.

Is.

A.

Stupid.

Improv.

Show.

It is possible, just possible, that what you did is one of the least important things that you will ever do in your life. You got on a platform and made up words! That's what you are now so angry and crazy about. Making up dumb words!

What? Isn't it perfectly acceptable to have notes and talk about a show after? Yes, but it's an improv show. As with all things improvisation, it depends on *how* you do it and what's motivating the discussion.

First of all, I'm a huge advocate of the fact *that* you did an improv show. Celebrate first that you did it, no matter how it went. You created an entire show out of absolutely nothing, and that's a lot to celebrate. That is amazing, in and of itself.

Now think of a time when your group had a great show. A show that just killed. Think of what you all did after that show. High fives, hugs, laughs, nods, shared mutual feelings of elation, completion, exhaustion, and joy. Did your group then go to a table and look at every single scene that you just performed, dissecting it moment by moment, looking at every single step along the way, analyzing why it went well here and what move made sense there and what laugh propelled the next moment and the next laugh, and then looking at the intricate construction and destruction of the success, etc.? I bet you didn't. I bet you had a beer and celebrated. I bet that you kind of just crossed it off as a miracle. I bet you can't even remember exactly what happened, and any "notes" you gave each other were just memories of the shit you did that killed.

This is very different than if the show sucked. When it sucks, you remember everything. You actually sit down and go through every moment of every scene and talk about what went wrong. All night long...

Have you ever thought about why your group can talk about a bad show for an hour, but when you have a good show, it is just checked off as great? Have you ever wondered why you can remember so much about a bad show, but seemingly very little about a great one?

First of all, I believe that you can't remember a great show because your right brain is "winning" and keeping your left brain busy. When you are improvising, either the right, playful, creative, intuitive part of your brain is dominating your thinking in the scene, or the left, intellectual, analytical part of your brain is. If the creative side is "winning," the analytical side becomes a "slave" to the playful side.

For example, if you whimsically declare your character in a scene to be "overreactive guy," then your left brain—the intellectual side—is busily thinking of choices to bring more heat, power, or heightened fun to the choice of "overreactive." That part of your brain just keeps thinking, "Must have more things for overreactive guy to react to! Must engage more." And that's *all* it is doing in what is probably a pretty fun scene. That strait-laced, protective, intellectual side is in on the fun of the other side of your brain's creation, using its way of thinking to fuel the fun point of view. After the scene, your left brain can't remember much about how the scene went or what happened. It was too "wrapped up in it all." Often in spite of itself.

In a bad, boring scene, the thinking part of your brain isn't feeding anything more powerful than an assessment of what is going on in your actual experience. If no truly fun choices are being produced, the intellectual side of the brain is able to think things like, "What is going on in the scene?" and "Why did I just say that?" It is analyzing the improvisation, not feeding and fueling a funny, great choice or a playful point of view. No wonder it can then remember *every* single bad thing that happened in the scene and recall it later.

This is the difference between the "in the zone" feeling of a good improv show versus the "in your head," sluggish, awful feeling of a bad one. Of course you can sit around for an hour dissecting every scene. You had a stoic computer—your brain—clinically documenting every moment of every scene, and the fact that it was doing that is, ironically, why the show was bad in the first place.

Understanding this relationship between what your left brain was doing and how much of the show you can recall is a good first step to managing notes after an improv show. Simply remain aware that there is a correlation. It wasn't really a "miracle" that the good show was so fun. It was because the ensemble's mind was together in a particular place, sharing a way of being or thinking. That's why you have a hard time remembering the show. As far as your brain is concerned, it just *was*.

I am not telling you, "Never do notes after an improv show." I am saying, "Don't do notes after an improv show in that dissecting way." It is not fun, and it is a waste of time.

If you have to do notes after an improv show, keep it light and keep it short. Look at behavior, not at every single moment of each scene wondering what could have or should have been done. Patterns of behavior that can affect the next show are the most valuable notes to address, not a flow chart of each scene's mistakes or a list of better choices.

"We are doing too many angry scenes. Let's keep an eye on that," is a behavioral pattern that an improviser can wrap his brain around and do something about next week.

"What should she have done in the park scene when the guy walked up?" is useless and anger-invoking. It doesn't give a player anything she can use to improve her next performance. It is only a clinical recount of a specific choice.

As a matter of fact, when I give improv notes, I only use specific scene examples to highlight or recall the *behavior* of which I speak. It is never really about missed, wrong, or better choices, just behavioral observations.

Directors of improv groups sometimes conduct these excruciating note sessions because they feel like that is what they are supposed to do, or they don't know how to look for performance patterns that they could address instead. I invite all of us to look at the weight we place on post-show improv notes and pull it back. Relax a bit and don't take them so seriously. Truly celebrate that you did what you set out to do. Better yet, minimize the time you and your ensemble rip a show apart with detailed notes and maximize the time spent discussing the good things you did.

If you have a rehearsal coming up in the next week, think about letting the notes rest until that rehearsal. I know some say that you should give notes "while it is still fresh and new," but I say that is overrated and people will remember more than you think. If they don't, or if it doesn't seem like a relevant point anymore, then in my opinion that note really wasn't necessary. It's a valuable and easy way to pare down the amount of notes. I always look at the time between a show and a rehearsal as an opportunity for the director to look at his notes with greater scrutiny and eliminate some of them. This streamlines the rehearsal, saving time just for notes with great clarity and purpose.

SPLIT SCENES

I can tell a hell of a lot about improvisers from the way they manage and perform in split scenes. Just to clarify, a split scene is when two or more separate groups of people, traditionally two sets of two, are doing two different scenes at the same time onstage. There is usually a back and forth of dialogue, taking turns doing a bit of each scene.

The first thing I notice is when and how an improviser recognizes that a split scene is happening in a long form. A lot of people *freak out* when a split scene starts. There is usually an odd overlap of dialogue, verbal and physical stops, and stutters. Determining when a split scene is happening is really quite simple and worthy of any ensemble's rehearsal time. The easy indicator is that if someone stays after an edit, it's probably going to be a split scene. If you make a fairly obvious edit to a scene, and the people from the last scene stay onstage on purpose, then it is probably going to be a scene that shares focus. In other words, a split scene. The reason there are quite often stops and stutters, especially among new groups, is that there is a moment of judgment that comes after the edit. The person editing a scene may go through a half-second pause, wondering why the previous scene's players are still there. Did they not catch the edit? It takes the editing player a while to process the idea of a split scene, and that hesitation creates the awkward sputter. Rehearse split scenes so you are familiar with them and thus not thrown into these situations.

If you are in a scene when an edit occurs and your scene partner decides to initiate a split scene instead of leaving, how do you know? Your scene partner makes the choice to stay. That is simply how you know. A savvy improviser will think, "Okay, split scene." A newer one will think, "What just happened? Should I stay? What? What the *hell* is going on?" and miss dialogue and timing in the process.

If a split scene is launched with all parties immediately oriented to and comfortable with what is happening, then it has a much better chance of keeping its appropriate momentum.

The momentum itself is the second thing I look at in the execution of split scenes. Are they keeping the rhythm of the scenes together? Quite often, in one of the two scenes, the players will talk their scene to death, never giving the focus over to the other scene. There is a certain finesse in knowing to hand focus over to the other scene after six point one lines of dialogue. Similarly, the other scene has to then know when to take that focus. If they are properly offered it, great, but if not, they have to learn to take it. This is simple give and take in improvisation. Half the time each half gives, and half the time each half takes. Give and take balances improvisation and keeps it on its toes. Split scenes are the prince of this idea. Like silence, if the give and take is not properly balanced, the inequality becomes the default declaration, and it becomes hard to break out of it.

Speaking of silence, the third indicator of an improviser's savvy and experience is what she does when her scene isn't the focus. A novice improviser will ferociously mime dialogue to the other person in the scene. This is distracting and looks stupid. Another tactic is to completely freeze and remain frozen until it is time for that scene to resume. This is fine, as long as it is the ensemble's consensus of what to do in a split scene. If so, then it looks good, choreographed, and chosen. Often this isn't the case, though, and one person kind of freezes with the other player not quite freezing, then freezing, and both looking at each other and freezing, then not.

The thing to do if a consensus has not been discussed is to perform "quiet business," or slight physical activity related to your scene, in a very subtle way. You get bonus points if you occasionally look at your scene partner to keep yourselves connected in whatever point of view, emotion, or attitude you may possess in the scene, but not so much that it creates a layer of silent tension.

EXERCISE

Remember the two-line editing exercise? Do this with split scenes, two lines at a time. Let the scenes go for about twenty lines, alternating ten exchanges of two lines each. It's tough, but it will really ingrain the rhythm of split scenes and the necessary give and take. The pace of the lines will get right where it needs to be, picking up in the middle of the previous thought or line and continuing with great momentum forward.

I have directed structured long forms where I choreographed just these moments in the form, where something triggers two two-person split scenes with two lines a piece and no interruptions, and then is edited out. It is like a machine gun placed in the middle of the long form, and does a great job of restoring the pace and breaking up linear stretches in the show.

WRITING WITH LONG FORM

I use improvisation all the time as a tool to write sketch comedy at The Second City, as well as narrative and sketch comedy at The Annoyance. However, there are two improvisational constructs that I have had little luck with when it comes to writing sketch. In particular, those constructs are short games, like Freeze Tag, and long form that is in continuum or references itself.

On the game side, the construct of something like Freeze Tag often prevents it from being anything sustainable outside the protection of its attributes. If you take any slice, segment, or scene out of the Freeze Tag context, then it isn't usually a comedic event in and of itself. For example, it doesn't really make sense to say the word "Clear!" without transitioning from the player holding flares guiding airplanes onto a runway to the new player holding defibrillators. It's that sudden transformation that makes Freeze Tag scenes work. If you used this scene outside of that context, you would merely have a scene that starts with the action of trying to save someone's life with defibrillators. It would be another scene based on another thing, which is fine, but Freeze Tag really didn't help it develop. As much as we might like to talk about the noble version of Freeze Tag being a scenic experience, it does rely on its device to propel it.

The performers play Freeze Tag at the end of every set at The Second City, and when I'm directing, it may seem like a good idea for me to stay and watch it to maybe get a kernel of an idea or a "good character." Unfortunately (fortunately), I've learned over the years that I don't get sketch material from Freeze Tag. It is what it is, and that's why it works. So I've also learned that it is a good cue for me to go to the bar and order a delicious Glenlivet on the rocks.

Finding sketch material in long form is also very difficult. As I said, long form is often "in continuum," or references itself, which makes it a hard thing from which to mine sketch scenes, though I've tried. Boy, have I tried.

A lot of long form is transformational, and that is what I mean by "continuum." It morphs or transforms into the next thing, often being fairly episodic or slow in its performance. This usually creates a less "packaged" scene. Let's say, for example, that you have a scene idea and you'd like to improvise it in an improv set, the way that The Second City would test material in a show process. The person with the idea might have a premise, a location, a character or two in mind, and perhaps already know what the scene is about. While certainly not perfect, the scene is at least approached with the packaged product in mind. I don't mean this in a gross commercial way, just a more structured beginning, middle, and end way. The scene strives for an arc that has been given some consideration beforehand.

Well, a lot of scenes in long form, by nature, don't have those kind of packaged builds, arcs, and outs. They are, as I said, a bit more episodic and transform more gradually. This is not a bad thing for long form as an approach to performing a piece of improvisation. In fact, it's quite wonderful. It just makes it difficult to pick out the individual scenes as their own distinct product possibility for a show. It is not impossible, just hard. Add to that the thinking in the minds of the performers with callbacks, themes, tag outs, etc., and the show is often impenetrable to content mining. It is, instead, an individual, "once in a lifetime" improv performance piece. It is difficult to recreate. It is difficult to extract any one element. It is amorphous and fluid.

If I do use long form to create possible sketch scenes, it is usually with the help of a construct that encourages a series of truly unrelated scenes. If it is a live improv set, then I'll use perhaps a Jim Game or a Pad Set, where the players take a bunch of suggestions from the audience and pull from them throughout the improv set. There can be full scenes, some mini-montage pieces, or a full long form based on a single suggestion or many suggestions along the way. The reason I like this is that it eliminates the *need* for continuous transformational improvisation that references itself and allows for other kinds of scenic, packaged improvisation instead. If performed in front of an audience, I might also encourage a Commando Set, where the players take suggestions along the way and immediately improvise based on the theme at the time. This also encourages improvisation that is more compartmentalized with singular scenic focus. In the end, it is easier to extract a particular scenic entity than an element that is more reliant on a larger, flowing, ever-changing whole.

If I am in a rehearsal scenario, as opposed to an improv set before a live audience, I might gravitate toward a montage of scenes based on a single suggestion. I have done this many times, either self-edited by the cast or edited by me. Sometimes I'll put a time limit on each scene. In a rehearsal, we may do sixty scenes in a half hour, each scene being thirty seconds long. The time element, along with the unrelated nature of the scenes with absolutely no burden of connecting them and no need to transform or even worry about editing, usually creates a volume of packaged ideas and scenarios that become possibilities for future development. I say "volume" on purpose, because the development of sketch comedy is best served with a volume of ideas winnowed down to the select few. So I won't get fifty out of sixty scenes, but I might just get ten, which is a hell of a good half hour's work.

When you approach writing, think about how you are using long form and other games to create material. Identify the qualities of particular games and forms, and determine whether the context allows enough freedom to create individual pieces as candidates for a sketch or narrative show, or whether the structure is so dominant that without it the scene won't play at all.

DIFFERENT SCHOOLS OF IMPROVISATION

It is so hard to reconcile all of the different approaches to improvisation. From Keith Johnstone, to Del Close at The iO, to The Groundlings, to ComedySportz, to UCB and the PIT and Magnet, to The Second City, to The Annoyance... there are a lot of different influences and information.

I only have three things to say to all of that.

First, no matter what you learn, it always boils down to *how* you do it. You can learn this technique and that move, but the "how" is the thing that you bring to it—your own identity and your own unique point of view. How you do it is why it will be funny, as well. I believe that the "how" is the valuable constant, no matter what the influence.

Second, there is no right way to teach people to make up words. It is ridiculous, in my opinion, to think that there is only one way of teaching or one way of learning the concept of "making up any words you want onstage." It just isn't true, and it doesn't even make sense. If anyone were to believe that there is one correct approach, that person would essentially be saying, "You can say or do anything you want in the art of improvisation, but there is only *one way* to say or do anything you want to say or do, and it is *this* way." That is ludicrous.

Third, and I know it sounds boring because you hear it all the time about everything, I suggest you approach this with the age-old "take what you want from it" or "use what works for you." Dull, but also very true. There is *no one keeping score* of how much you use iO's approach or how much you use UCB's or Second City's approach. No one cares about your approach enough to monitor how much they see this or that influence in you. Sure, in a class or workshop, a particular instructor or director of a particular school of thought is looking at you through that particular lens. But it's only for that amount of time. After that experience, you really *do* get to choose for yourself and take what makes sense and actually makes a difference for you. That teacher isn't at your independent team rehearsal or at your performance of an improvised one act at Jimmy's Bar. That is *your time* to try stuff that works for you.

My entire school of thought comes from what works for me. That's all. If the idea of "rules" and "yes, and" is too restricting and gets you thinking in a bad way, then fuck The Second City. If you don't get enough power from "playing slow and near yourself," fuck iO. If you've tried and don't like the game construct of a UCB scene, then fuck it. If you make selfish choices at the top of a scene and it doesn't work for you, then fuck me and The Annoyance. Nobody is keeping score of what you do from which school or philosophy when you are *actually* performing.

Seriously, take what works. If you take what works for you, then it *works*, meaning that it is interesting and playful and probably funny while you are doing it. No one, including me, is going to be watching and laughing my ass off, saying, "Yeah, but it didn't really follow the structure of an Annoyance scene very well." No. It will just be funny, with whatever you bring to it that works.

It would be impossible to reconcile all of the different schools of thought on improvisation. To say that there is only one way of doing improv is dumb. Mike Nichols, Elaine May, Bill Murray, and Alan Arkin were all brilliant improvisers. How did they possibly do it? They had never heard of The Annoyance or iO or UCB or really anything. How did they manage without learning the "right" way to do it?

A FINAL THOUGHT

Competition between improv theaters is stupid. God knows I have participated in it, but I have also been fairly instrumental in curbing it a bit here in Chicago.

Why do you suppose such competition exists? Well, one reason is because each sketch-based and improv theater is reaching out to the same students and the same audience. Or at least it seems that way. It isn't really completely true, but it sure feels that way. Another reason is the "different schools of thought" discussion. We each like to think that our way is *the* way to do improv, so it breeds ownership about a particular philosophy or way of thinking. There are also the relative commercial and artistic perceptions of individual theaters that create a chasm. Perhaps this theater thinks that other one is selling out, or one is jealous of the other's commercial success and its ability to pay people, etc. It goes on and on. Finally, one last reason is the history between individual people in the community. This person used to work with that person, but they had a creative or business difference, so now, in response, they are going to do this or start that, etc.

Meanwhile, your typical, modern improviser/student/solo/sketch performer merely wants to bounce around from one great place to another as if the world is an improv amusement park, a stage here and a beer there, a comedy discussion here and a failed hookup there, with a stumble home here and there. These performers want an improv frolic in whatever city, learning through the culture, saturation, study, pain, and celebration what each school and venue has to offer. They become confused and a bit disinterested in anything regarding a feud, a past history, a competition, or bad blood between theaters. It really doesn't matter to them, as they have little need to be "right" or "hold on to" anything other than last night or the next show or the next PBR. The next good time.

The irony with all of this is evident to nearly every owner, artistic director, or instructor at each theater, but often the hubris and propriety remain. What is that irony? Really (yes really), everyone does better when there isn't the feeling of hierarchy among different organizations. We all know that students and audiences who are interested in this type of comedy and training are going to travel to all the schools and theaters, so anything that makes that exploration more difficult is actually a bad artistic and financial decision. Why bother making people feel bad for being a part of your organization or your competitor's? It really *only* makes people feel bad, because it isn't going to deter them.

Point is, take it from me, it is all stupid. I have enjoyed the evolution of the theaters' camaraderie here in Chicago over the last twenty-five years. It hasn't been a party all of the time, and there are still conflicts, but I do believe that everyone at least shares the attitude and actions associated with getting along and supporting each other, even with slips and barbs and jabs in between.

I really invite owners, artistic directors, instructors, and directors to take a good hard look at themselves in regard to this. The only thing this uninvited—and to be honest, elitist— philosophy helps to do is make students and performers feel bad, wrong, and guilty for wanting to enjoy one theater as much as they enjoy the next one. It hurts your goodwill, your working reputation, and your pocketbook.

That said, if you want to learn the right way to do it…

I'm kidding.

If in Chicago, stop and have a beer at The Annoyance, 851 West Belmont. There's also The Annoyance Theatre in Brooklyn, NY.

Thank you for reading this book about long form improvisational comedy. And scene.

AUTHOR BIOGRAPHY

FOUNDER AND VISIONARY behind the acclaimed Annoyance Theatre, Mick Napier is known both nationally and internationally as an innovator and creative force in comedy, improvisation, and theatre. His belief in the element of risk-taking that is at the core of improvisation influences his work and his direction, inspiring genuine creativity in any project with which he is involved.

With The Annoyance, Mick has spent more than twenty-five years developing and cultivating a style of work and production that has been both acclaimed and imitated. As a Director and Artistic Consultant for the internationally renowned Second

City, he made his mark, having directed more than ten revues there including the fortieth and fiftieth anniversary revues, and *Paradigm Lost*, which earned him a Joseph Jefferson Award for Direction. Throughout his career, Mick has directed such high profile actors and writers as Aidy Bryant and Vanessa Bayer (*Swear Jar*), Tina Fey, Jason Sudeikis, and Stephen Colbert (The Second City), Martin Short (*Martin Short & Friends*), Jeff Garlin (*I Want Someone to Eat Cheese With*), and David and Amy Sedaris in their Obie Award-winning hit *One Woman Shoe*.

In film, Mick directed and edited Annoyance Productions' first feature film, *Fatty Drives the Bus*, which was released by Troma Pictures in November 1999. For television, he was Writer/Performance Director for the Cable Ace nominated *Exit 57*, which aired on Comedy Central for two seasons and Creative Producer on the nationally syndicated sketch TV show *The Sports Bar*. His original animations have appeared on the cable programs *Tame Show* and *R-Rated*, as well as in the Chicago Comedy Film Festival.

As an actor, Mick has appeared in the films *Ice Harvest*, *Let's Go to Prison*, *Watch*, and *Talent*, and on television was himself as a talent judge in the Canadian reality show *Next Comedy Legend*. The PBS-aired documentary *Second to None* chronicles Mick's process of directing a show for The Second City. Mick has also worked with many companies and organizations over the past fifteen years in areas such as communication, collaboration, innovation, leadership, and presentation.

Mick's hobbies include card magic, lock picking, Erector Sets, pocket billiards, and collecting lighters. He also enjoys performing a mentalist act with his partner, Jennifer Estlin.